Whispers of Grace

Stories • Devotions • Poems • Prayers

Volume 2

SpeakUp Conference

Compiled by

Living Parables of Central Florida

D1260521

Whispers of Grace

Stories • Devotions • Poems • Prayers

Volume 2

ISBN: 978-1-952369-22-3

Published by EA Books Publishing a division of
Living Parables of Central Florida, Inc. a 501c3
EABooksPublishing.com

Living Parables of Central Florida, Inc., of which EABooks Publishing is a division, offers publishing contests at Christian conferences to provide opportunities for unpublished authors to be discovered and earn publishing credits. We publish high quality, self-published books that bring glory and honor to God's Kingdom.

ACKNOWLEDGMENTS

We'd like to thank Carol Kent and Bonnie Emmorey of the SpeakUp Conference for encouraging and equipping writers and speakers for the glory of the Kingdom of God. We wish to thank Cheri Cowell and her wonderful team at EABooks Publishing for giving us this opportunity. We thank our many friends and family for supporting us in our writing dreams. And most importantly, we want to thank our Lord and Savior Jesus Christ for His gifts—may this book bring you the honor and glory you deserve.

TABLE OF CONTENTS

Can you hear it? Life often gets in the way of us hearing it—the roar of doubt, fear, and despair drown out the still small voice. But if we tune our ear to hear, it is there. Whispers of grace come to us when we lend our ear to the movements of God in our struggles, in our everyday lives, and in our hearts. May these stories, prayers, and poems create in you a desire to listen for the whispers of grace in your own life.

SpeakUp Conference

In All Things, In Every Way

Jennifer Allen

Ah last night, my husband, my girls, and I went out for dinner. It had been a super stressful day for all of us.

"What brings you in tonight? Anything special?" our waitress asked.

"Our kitchen sink is sitting on our deck," I replied. Yep! *That* kind of stressful day.

As we gathered around the table at one of our favorite restaurants, it felt so nice to take a few minutes and catch our breath. Sitting there, waiting for my mushroom and alfredo pizza, I soaked in the faces around me. My oldest girls happily playing tic-tac-toe, my husband contentedly scrolling through his phone, my youngest scribbling away at an octopus on her menu. Stressful day aside, all of it together made me feel so happy.

When our lovely meal drew to an end and our bill arrived, we were in for a fabulous treat: unbeknownst to us, a kind stranger had generously paid for our dinner.

I've heard of people having this happen to them or kind souls doing this sort of thing for someone else but it's never happened to me or to us. How I wish I knew who our benefactor was. How I would so love to thank him or her.

What more could my husband and I do but shake our heads and smile and at least say, "Thank you, God."

On the way home, I explained to my girls what had happened and a memory popped into my mind.

Last fall, while playing at the park, what looked like a single mom and her two boys joined my girls on the playground. As we were leaving I couldn't help but notice her car. Busted out window, bungee cord holding the trunk shut, duck tape securing a taillight.

"Buy them lunch," the Still Small Voice whispered.

Say again?

"Buy them lunch."

Really?

"Really."

Oh, but that would be awkward, and weird, and the kind of social situation that is totally out of my comfort zone . . .

"Buy them lunch."

Okay, okay, if you say so . . .

A few minutes later my girls and I returned to the park with Happy Meals in hand. It felt a little strange but a whole lot of good to watch the young mom call her boys over to the bench where she was sitting. The surprise and joy on all their faces was worth every twitch of awkward and weird I might have felt.

"Remember that day we brought lunch to that family at the park?" I asked my oldest, recalling the memory to her mind too.

"Yeah," she said.

"You can *never* out-give God. We bought that family a couple of Happy Meals, but tonight God blessed *our* family with that big, beautiful meal we just enjoyed."

"What do you mean?" she countered, still a little confused.

"A stranger, someone we don't even know, paid for our dinner tonight, and I believe God was using him or her to bless us."

Understanding spread over her face, and I could tell she was experiencing a whole new dimension of God's love. If that doesn't rival the sweetest of desserts, I don't know what does.

Later that night, when all four of my girls were tucked in tight and my husband was sound asleep, I couldn't stop thinking of the unexpected gift we'd been given. I started to consider not just the blessing but all that went into making it happen.

All the things that went both wrong and right throughout our day to land us at that restaurant . . .

All that must have gone into everything on the end of our kind stranger to make him or her do such an incredible thing . . .

I even thought of the fine-tuning that must have gone on behind the scenes that day at the park. Things that happened before and after that I will never know.

Our weeknight dinner surprise was so much more than a blessing; it was an intricate display of God's love for us.

I recently saw something on Facebook that sent me into a tizzy. A friend of mine posted something about an exciting event in her life that I would very much like to see happen in mine. I felt jealous. *Nauseously* jealous. The post . . .the pictures that went with the post . . . the dream come true for her and not for me. It seemed so unfair.

But if God can intricately weave together a Thursday night dinner in order to bless me and show me His unfathomable love, how much more must He be weaving, and painting, and writing an incredibly elaborate love story for me? A grand romance. A fairy tale. Complete with generous strangers, and boys with Happy Meals, and countless dreams of my own come true.

In C.S. Lewis's *The Horse and His Boy*, Shasta becomes distraught over something he sees happening to Aravis. But Aslan tells him, "I'm telling you *your* story, not hers," reminding him not to get so caught up in someone else's business that he misses what Aslan is doing in his.

It's one of my favorite passages, and when I find myself in a jealous spin cycle, it helps me so much to remember that God is crafting a story just for me, and this story is all that matters.

God's love for us is so, so big, but it's also incredibly small.

It's intricate.

His love, His plan, and His purpose are poured into every detail. It goes right down to our core, into our cells, into our very atoms, as my science-loving friend, Jessie, would say.

He's everywhere, in everything. Declaring His message over and over and over again . . .

"I love you."

"I love you."

"In all things. In every way . . ."

"I."

"Love."

"You."

Jennifer Allen is a writer, reader, and librarian at heart. Married for seventeen years, she feels lucky to live in Michigan and adores homeschooling her own set of "Little Women." Jennifer is currently working on a novel for fairytale lovers and a nonfiction book for homeschooling moms.

Garments of Grief

Peg Arnold

There is a time for everything and a season for every activity under the heavens: a time to be born and a time to die, a time to weep and a time to laugh, a time to mourn and a time to dance.
Ecclesiastes 3:1, 2, 4 NIV

The death of someone we love can be devastating. Every time it happens, we find ourselves on a different path of grief. How we grieve is often influenced by circumstances surrounding the loss. Sometimes the death follows a long illness and is expected; or it could be an untimely death that completely destroys all that is familiar, forcing us to find a new normal. No matter how many times we have experienced the grieving process, we discover new challenges with each loss. It is in God's Word where we can discover the strength and grace that provide us hope and comfort. *He has sent me to bind up the brokenhearted, to comfort all who mourn* (Isaiah 61:1b-2 NIV).

My personal losses have ranged from the sudden, unexpected death of a parent, to suicide, to illnesses, including the arduous journey of dementia with many difficult good-byes in between. With every single death, there was no way to prepare my soul for that final good-bye. When I was grieving the loss of my mom, I felt the voice of God whisper new insights. His message was filled with grace and helped me understand the healing process of grief symbolized by garments. The assurance and words He gave me continue to provide hope and support for each challenging moment.

The Garments of Grief

Death is the ruthless thief that rips away a vibrant spirit at the most unexpected time.

Death is the uninvited visitor that lurks in the corners

and leaves with a precious soul in spite of many prayers for healing.

Death is the expected and sometimes welcome guest that escorts a loved one up

the golden stairway to their heavenly Savior.

Whether you experience death as the thief, the uninvited visitor, or the guest,

Death always leaves a wardrobe of grief garments for those who remain behind.

The quilt of memories offers a refuge in lonely times

and sometimes lulls you back to sleep on those mornings it is hard to move.

The scratchy undergarment of despair makes every task difficult,

yet there is no easy way to remove it in exchange for another garment.

The hooded sweatshirt of avoidance allows you to disconnect from the world

and continue on as if nothing has happened.

The black shawl of sorrow exposes your grief to everyone in your life.

The heavy coat appears normal, but everywhere you go,

you carry the invisible, weighted burden of loss.

The shoes of shock provide a deceitful opportunity to run away from the truth of Death.

The healing robe is like a hug and provides security at the end of an exhausting day.

The wristwatch marks celebrations and memories,

as a constant reminder that your loss is permanent.

The mask of cheer conceals your anger, loneliness, and tears,

allowing you to pretend that everything is okay.

The suit of acceptance hides in the back corner.

You look at it now and then, but each time you try it on, it doesn't fit quite right, yet.

Each garment is neatly stored in the wardrobe that Death has provided, and wearing some or all of them is part of the grieving process. Some garments we choose to wear, other times the garment chooses us. Some garments lose their usefulness early, but others linger in the corners and we are caught by surprise when they appear.

The one raiment Jesus offers to us every morning is the garment of praise.

It is a promise of heaven's gift of reunion and hope for all those who believe in Jesus Christ. Isaiah the prophet reassures us that

the Lord *provides for those who grieve in Zion, to bestow on them a crown of beauty instead of ashes, the oil of joy instead of mourning, and a garment of praise instead of a spirit of despair* (Isaiah 61:3 NIV).

Wherever you are in your journey of grief, I pray you try on the garment of praise and embrace the hope and grace provided by our Lord Jesus Christ.

Dear Lord, When I rise each morning and go to bed each night. Help me to seek your strength, comfort, and wisdom, as I travel through this season of grief. I thank you for my loved one's life, their gifts, their faith, and their legacy. I pray for those I know who are also walking this difficult path of grief. Surround them with grace, comfort, and strength to face each day. Amen

Peg Arnold brings stories to life in her engaging speaking ministry that encourages all to embrace their God-given value. As a church leader, mom to two adult children, and nana to five, she freely shares her life experiences and how Christ revealed His hope and love for all.

Wings of Grace

Terri Baxter

"The grace of our lord flowed out superabundantly and beyond measure for me."[2]

I was marveling at the brilliance of the central Oregon sky as I walked my trail. Not a wisp of a jet stream or cloud as far as I could see. My eyes delighted at the contrast of the crystal blue sky and the brilliant green of the juniper tree ahead. I was gazing up at the tree when I came to a dead halt. Not more than five feet above me, he sat. Golden glass eyes. Silently I stood, barely breathing, not wanting to send him into flight. Most owls take off before you get too close. Why didn't he swoop away like all the others? I could see his strong talons clamped onto the tree branch, the

---

[1] Levi Lundy took this picture for me of the father owl in the tree

[2] 1 Timothy 1:14

pronounced feathers by the eyes as they drew up to tall tipped-like ears on each side of his head. The variations of grays, black, and white in the feathers. I spoke quietly, telling him how beautiful he was, then ever so carefully stepped forward to continue my walk.

Each day I would pass the tree. Each day he was there. Same tree. Same branch. Watching. I stopped to talk. He tolerated my presence with a perturbed, sleepy look. Then I continued on. Out of curiosity, I began looking into other trees. I didn't have to look far. The next tree over brought immediate understanding for this ever-present staunch guardian. He had a family. If dad was the guardian, mom was a no-nonsense gal, intimidating, tough, and with a glare that could buckle your knees. Four little puff balls of creamy down feathers; heads popped up, little eyes peeking above the woven work of branches, watching the world.

Photo by Levi Lundy.[3] Copyright Terri Baxter 2008

I found I could view their family right out my patio door. Meals were regular. I would watch as the mothers head would drop down to the bottom of the nest and arise with a sage rat, mole, mouse, or prairie dog. She stripped the meat using her beak and talons like skilled kitchen tools. Strip and dangle, strip and dangle, as each owlet reached for

---

[3] Levi Lundy took this picture for me of the mother owl and owlets

its meal. When they finished eating that critter, she dipped back down to the nested pantry for the second course. Over and over throughout the day this routine went on.

Then flight school began. The owlets, at first, sat in the nest flapping their wings. Next, they were stepping out onto the edges of the nest, then making their way out onto supporting branches, working and moving those wings constantly. The fun started when they began to frolic, fluttering and flitting in short hop-flights through the branches of the tree. I found myself giggling out loud as the rookie pilots and navigators collided into each other. As the lighter branches bounced with the weight of their bodies, they hung tightly with their little talons, swaying with the boughs. By dusk, they clustered and cuddled back at the nest. This was their safe haven and their training ground, their life revolved around this tree that was home.

It was the storms that caught my attention most. I would lay in bed at night hearing the wind howl, rain pelting down as spring storms passed through. I wondered how the owl family was. The babies, vulnerable and weak. Then came the hail. It was the size of golf balls. I could see it coming, making its way across the pasture. The sound as it hit the roof and patio was deafening; the force puncturing a two-inch hole right through the heavy plastic tray on the outdoor BBQ.

Isn't that like life? Coming out of nowhere. Storms hitting with force and destruction. Will I make it through another chemo treatment, another surgery? The addiction seems to be winning. The betrayal devastates. The pain unbearable. How long will this virus hold on? My savings is running out. Can my business make it another month? The storms hit hard.

My thoughts went to the owlets, so fragile. Their home didn't have a roof or branches overhead. One hit by the hail could be fatal. Hurriedly one night, I grabbed my binoculars to view their life in the storm. My heart was moved with compassion and respect. There, covering the nest with her body and wings, sat the mother owl. The hail pounded; she took the blows. The storm ravaged all around her. She was immoveable, impenetrable. The storm would have to pass through her first. "Oh," I gasped. "Jesus, that's you on the cross. That's you in the storms with us, through the battering this world brings. Your grace covering us like the wings of the mother owl in the storm. Wings of Grace."

Sheltered under the mother's wings. Engulfed, nestled in the plush, thick softness of hundreds of down feathers, the owlets were protected. The outside storm was hushed, muffled to a whisper. A quiet calm resided in their refuge. This is God's covering of grace, soft as down feathers we are nestled.[4] The storm rages, yet God's grace holds us through the storm. Later, the sun came out, the hail passed. Checking the nest, I counted; one, two, three, all four little heads popped up, peeking out. Mom was gone. Hunting no doubt. Dinner can't wait. Some things never change.

Storms are not held back from life. Some seasons hit with force, unrelenting. It was one day among many in what had been a long and difficult season that my ninety-two-year-old father took a turn. Like the owlets, his body was weak and vulnerable. The paramedics had been out just two days before. They and the doctors gave us medical advice to follow at home to keep Dad from going to the hospital amid the COVID virus. Two days later, there was a drastic change. My mom went to change from her bed clothes as I came to sit beside Dad. It was all happening so fast. Dad's eyes closed, complexion pale, breaths shallow. Knowing what we may be facing, I held Dad's hands and prayed for God to be with us.

Time stood still. The only sounds the ticking of the big grandfather clock. I watched for his chest to rise and fall. "Was that his last breath?"

---

[4] Ps. 57:1 God covers us under His wings until the storms of destruction pass

I had made the call to the paramedics once again. It was a twenty-minute drive for them. Would Dad make it? The 9-1-1 operator broke in. "Ma'am, stay on the line, the paramedics are on their way. I will stay on with you." The dispatcher kept me on the phone, but my mind and spirit were speaking to God. "Jesus, is it Dad's time? Are you taking him home today?" My heart was mixed. A feeling of privilege to usher Dad into God's Kingdom, along with the reality of the loss of my dad's presence on this earth--this loving, witty man whom I had always admired and learned so much from. I didn't know what the next moments would bring. Dad was not responsive. Sitting close, my hand on his leg. Relief came as I saw his chest rise. It seemed like forever before the next gasp would come.

Music always soothed Dad's soul, and in difficult times music was our solace, playing songs of worship beckoning God's spirit into our midst.

With one hand holding the phone and my other hand resting on Dad, I tried to sing a worship song, but the words would not come. Barely able, I began to hum. The 9-1-1 operator quiet amidst this hallowed silence that now permeated the room. The grandfather clock ticked. I hummed the old hymns. Waiting. Watching.

"Ma'am, you should see the paramedics pulling in now." Came the quiet voice . . .

Dad came home from the hospital three days later. Doctors amazed at his quick recovery for his age. Surviving congestive heart failure, pneumonia, and a worsened heart condition.

God's grace came to us quietly that day, in the soft gentle humming of worship and a sacred silence. The outside storm was hushed, muffled to a whisper. A quiet calm resided.[5] Not a calm I could explain or a refuge we

---

[5] Mark 4:35-41 reminiscent of Jesus calming the storm in the boat with the disciples

deserved. This was God's covering of grace, soft as down feathers we were nestled, secure in this storm wrapped in His wings of grace.

"The grace of our lord flowed out superabundantly and beyond measure for me." [6]

God is with us. Always! Terri

Terri Baxter is the director of Healing Helps Ministry on staff at Powell Butte Church. She is the owner of BrainBalance, helping clients through her advanced certification as a Neurofeedback trainer. Terri's writings come from her experiences with family, ministry, business, and her exposure to the abundance of outdoor nature.

---

[6] 1 Timothy 1:14

Ruthless

Mary Harrington Chism

From the day she was born, in the hot midsummer of 1950, Ruth Lorraine Stacy was destined for Hollywood. Until she lost her "it" factor.

The eight-and-a-half months prior to Ruthie's birth were a time of grueling decision-making for her mother, Ruby, a confused and utterly selfish woman. Ruby openly toyed with the deep affections of two men, neither of whose names filled the "father" blank on Ruthie's birth certificate. It remained empty.

That previous autumn, Ruby had fled New Jersey for the South. Alone. Several years before, she had married Charles Stacy and moved north with him. Now, at twenty-three, she was the mother of his two young boys, whom she coldly abandoned, along with their father. A quick divorce should rid her of Charles, her sons, and an overbearing mother-in-law. That would fix those early mistakes.

Once back home, Ruby reconnected with her high school sweetheart, Robert Martin. She began to seduce him as a likely second husband. Several carefree weeks later, however, around Halloween, Ruby's mornings became fraught with sickness. *Not again.* Since she didn't know for certain who the father was, she decided she must keep the secret to herself—in case the baby had curly, red hair. Ruby ran again, heading from her small hometown to the obscurity of a large city, Memphis.

Situated in a working-class section of the Bluff City, the Bethany Home offered a timely refuge for Ruby. In this well-tended haven for unwed mothers—her still-binding marriage to Charles yet another secret—she lived, lied, and grew for months. She felt safe within those walls, her past in her past, until it drew near to the time she would become two.

What would she do with the baby?

Ruby needed to solve The Problem quickly. Her escape plan included finalizing the divorce from Charles, thus squelching any notion of going back to New Jersey with her little surprise. She dared not return to her Middle Tennessee family and risk alienation from them, or from Robert. She could see no way forward with a baby in tow.

Ruby's brilliant solution? She simply would not have a baby.

She would give away her third child, and no one would be the wiser. Problem solved.

And none too soon, as Ruthie arrived early. She was perfect, with ruddy flailing arms and legs, a robust cry, and as near bald as a proper lady should be. With no hint of hesitation, Ruby signed over her maternal rights to the Tennessee Children's Home Society, foregoing even a farewell touch, and left her daughter behind.

Miss Georgia Tann, the domineering head of the TCHS, nurtured high hopes for the bright-eyed orphan's future and even bigger dreams for her own wallet. She hurriedly arranged for Ruthie's adoption by a Hollywood celebrity couple known and loved by all America. They would provide this baby with everything money could buy. And the thought of the referrals her adoption would generate made Miss Tann dizzy.

Ruthie passed everything on the pre-flight checklist with excellent marks—except for her weight. Fearing Miss Tann's displeasure, the workers at the Home tried desperately to fatten her up. Although healthy for a preemie, Ruthie just could not attain the five-pound minimum limit required by the departure date. Clandestine air coach shipments by

16

basket to California did adhere to certain high standards, after all.

Deemed unsuitable for such arduous travel, Ruthie's prized status was suddenly downgraded to damaged goods. The girl destined for Hollywood suffered yet another great loss—the role of a lifetime, which now would be awarded to someone else's castaway. Ruthie's removal from her A-list was the only viable option for Miss Tann.

At three weeks old, Ruth Lorraine Stacy ceased to exist.

A few miles away, a long-married yet childless couple was enjoying a visit on the lawn with neighbors from another apartment. At around 8:00 p.m., they heard their phone ringing through the open screen door. It was the call they prayed for: "Mr. Hawley? Hurry over—we have your baby." Although lacking a crib and blankets, diapers and formula, dash over they did.

At three weeks old, Helen Marie Hawley came to be.

In a plot twist outrageously similar to the films of Tinseltown, divine intervention transformed the staggering losses of "Ruthie" into mighty blessings for "Helen." She grew plump and blossomed into a loving child, enjoying laughter among many friends, a superior education, cherished church traditions, a warm and close extended family, and genuinely loving parents. In a natural extension of her adoptive father's unconditional love—obvious to everyone—Helen would welcome without reservation our heavenly Father's offering of His greater love through Jesus.

God also became Abba to the once fatherless child, now twice chosen. In His sovereign grace, He assigned her to His A-list, securing her eternal destiny—not in Hollywood, but in heaven.

Life as an only child was never dull. I received all my parents' love and didn't have to share my toys. My "secret garden" was school, a source of many friendships vibrant today. Life—college, career, marriage, children—became even more joyous when Jesus entered it as my BFF.

I Need Graaaaace!

Beth L. Dutton

"Out of His fullness, we have all received His grace . . ."
John 1:16

I was curled up in my chair with my eyes closed, snatching a quick rest while my four-year-old daughter was in her room taking a nap. Or so I thought. I awoke to the sound of something crashing. Startled, I jumped up and ran to her room, afraid of what I might find when I got there.

With my hand on the door I pushed.

And prodded.

And pressed.

Peeking through the crack I finally created, I could see the debris of books scattered everywhere. The shelf was broken and tipped over on its side, holding back the door.

In the midst of the chaos sat my "sleeping" child, clutching to her chest a book that had been at the top of the bookshelf. One look at my face and she knew she was in trouble.

"Grace!" she pleaded with me. "I need graaaaace!"

Grace in our home is a word we use when any person, including the adults, know they are in trouble but end up not having to pay the consequences. We call it "giving grace." It's where the recipient receives undeserved favor.

The reality of life is that we all need grace. Even King Manasseh. King Manasseh ruled over Judah in Old Testament times. He wasn't just bad, he was evil. He built pagan altars in the Temple of the LORD, he practiced witchcraft and consulted with psychics. He murdered many innocent people until "Jerusalem was filled from one end to the other with innocent blood" (2 Kings 21:16).

But perhaps the most disturbing thing is that he actually sacrificed his own sons in the fire to the god Moloch. It is hard to imagine anyone more evil than that.

The Lord spoke to Manasseh, but he ignored the warnings. Finally, God "had enough!" He sent the Assyrian armies after him. They put a ring through his nose, bound him in chains, and led him away.

Good. He got what he deserved. End of story. Right? Wrong.

"While in deep distress, Manasseh sought the Lord and sincerely humbled himself before God. When he prayed, the Lord listened to him and was moved by his request. So, Manasseh was brought back to Jerusalem and to his kingdom. He finally realized that the Lord alone is God!" (2 Chronicles 33:12-13)

We all have sinned. Yet God says: "I have swept away your sins like a cloud. I have scattered your offenses like the morning mist. Oh, return to Me, For I have paid the price to set you free" (Isaiah 44:22).

The price He paid was not "mere gold or silver, which lose their value. It was the "precious blood of Christ, the sinless, spotless Lamb of God" (I Peter 1:18b-19).

God's grace.

Who can comprehend it? It is available to anyone who sincerely calls upon Him. If God can extend grace to someone like Manasseh, there is no one beyond His love and grace.

Ask yourself:

In what area of my life right now do I need God to extend His grace, His "undeserved favor?" Who in my life needs to know and experience God's grace? Who in my life needs me to show them grace?

Prayer of blessing:

May our Lord Jesus Christ and God the Father, who loves you and by His grace gives you eternal encouragement and good hope, encourage your heart and strengthen you in every good deed and word. Amen.

(Based on 2 Thessalonians 2:16-17)

Beth Dutton is a storyteller, seeker of adventure, lover of music, lover of Scripture, and most importantly, loved by God. She is married to fellow-adventurer Neal and mother hen to two grown chicks and a baby grand chick. Her earthly residence is in Minnesota. Her eternal residence is in heaven — the ultimate adventure!

God's Loving Embrace

Rachel Britton

My husband and I bought our young adult daughter a pair of noise-cancelling headphones as a Christmas gift. The large white pads that covered each ear made her look like she was from outer space. The headphones claimed to block out all distractions. If you wore them walking down a busy street, you could enjoy music as if you were standing in front of a band at a concert without the disturbance of traffic noise and beeping horns.

Our daughter brought these headphones with her when she moved back home to self-quarantine during the COVID-19 pandemic. They were a permanent attachment on her head from the moment she got up until she went to bed, whether she was working on her laptop or slouched on the sofa watching Netflix videos. "Noise-cancelling" allowed her to enjoy whatever she was doing free from the distraction of activities around her, and from requests for her attention. Often, I would call her name a number of times, "Phoebe . . . Phoebe . . . Phoebe," without any response. She would not be aware of my presence unless I waved my arms frantically and jumped up and down. Then, from the corner of her eye, the movement would catch her attention and she would look up. Or I would stand directly in front of her motioning with my hand by pointing to my mouth that I was trying to talk to her. She would remove her headphones with a smile, apologize, and ask me to repeat what I was saying.

Trying to get my daughter's attention makes me think of how often our heavenly Father tries to do the same with us, His children. In Isaiah 65:1-2 (GW), God says to His people: "Here am I, here am I . . . I stretched out my hands all day long to stubborn people. They chose to go the wrong direction. They followed their own plans." But they did not listen to Him. Instead, they chose to ignore Him and continued to do their own thing. It was like they were wearing noise-cancelling headphones.

Yet, God in His goodness promises that when people turn to Him, He will answer immediately. "Before they even call out to me, I will answer them; before they've finished telling me what they need, I'll have already heard" (Isaiah 65:24 TPT). God is waiting on the sidelines, ready to respond generously and shower love and mercy on those who repent.

Jesus told a story that gives a similar illustration of God's love and mercy. In Luke 15, a father patiently waited, on constant lookout, for his son to return home: "From a long distance away, his father saw him coming," says Luke 15:20 (TPT). The son had his confession rehearsed, but his father interrupted him in the middle of and "swept him up in his arms, hugged him dearly, and kissed him over and over with tender love" (Luke 15:20 TPT).

Often, we're no different from the people of Israel or the prodigal son. We get so busy with our day-to-day living that we forget to give God our attention. Or we leave Him out of our lives because we choose to ignore Him and do our own thing. Yet, God in His mercy is always ready and willing to respond to us with love and graciousness when we turn to Him.

I am reminded of a time when God didn't hesitate to show me His love and grace, even though I had disregarded Him. Distracted by my career and friends, I gradually left God out of my life. I slept in on Sunday mornings instead of going to church. Day after day, my Bible remained unopened. It wasn't until my husband and I moved to a different country for his work that, with the distractions gone, I finally thought about God. In a place where I knew no one, and without family or friends around me or work to fill my day, I turned to God for help. Immediately, I sensed He had responded to my prayer and embraced me as His child. God had been waiting with open arms calling, "Here I am, here I am," unable to be involved in my life until I invited Him in.

What about your own situation? God wants to have an active part in your life. Can you hear Him calling, "Here I am, here I am?" It doesn't have to be a high-flying career or a lively social life that keeps you distracted. Maybe keeping on top of demands for your time from family, ferrying children to and from after-school activities, or juggling work and home life is enough to keep you from prioritizing your relationship with God. Perhaps you've let your commitment to attending church regularly slip. You mean to have a quiet time each morning but somehow it never happens.

Now is the perfect time to take off your noise-cancelling headphones that have stopped you from hearing God calling to you, and turn your heart to him with a simple prayer, "Lord, I'm sorry." God in His love and mercy willingly responds. He will embrace you with open arms, give you a fresh new start, and celebrate that you have come back to Him.

Rachel is a British-born writer and speaker with a master's in religion from Gordon-Conwell Theological Seminary. Through her nonprofit, Rachel operates RADIANT.NYC, a community empowering young women in NYC, and reNEW, a retreat for writers and speakers in New England. Rachel cannot live without a mug of English tea.

Grace Garden

Kim Cusimano

A perennial, hardy seed,

Planted and germinated at the plea,

"God, save me."

Rooted in Calvary dirt,

Resilient in a wilting world,

It sprouts continually.

Not requiring a season,

Nor drop of water,

Or even a ray of sun.

It buds in childlike,

Finger-painted pots,

In cracked circumstances too.

Anticipated spring and summer blooms,

Yet such splendor in winter,

On days so cold and blue.

It flourishes unexpectedly,

No matter topsoil parched and dry,

The Gardener sees it with a different eye.

He is patient,

Gentle of hand,

Commands the rain.

He cultivates,

Prunes away self,

Pulls weeds and leaves His seeds.

With unmerited favor,

Underserved kindness,

He gardens and grows.

Creating a lush soul,

A barren to life-giving space,

A heart garden of flowering grace!

Kim Cusimano is a wife and mother to four. As a mother to two special-needs adults, she spends her time encouraging those around her to reach their full potential. In her free time, she enjoys writing poetry and articles that reflect the goodness of God.

Boxed In

S. M. Bungalow

Where shall I go, where shall I turn?
I am boxed in and fear there's no way out.
I am boxed in and I see no way out.
For months a race has been run, Hope as its fuel.
Always moving, but still blocked.

I am boxed in; I fear there is no way out.
I am boxed in; I see no way out.
I scream, I shout and say, "Let me out!"
I sense Christ is near and gently responds, "Not yet."

I am boxed in; I see no way out.
I am boxed in; there might be a way out.
2019 was hard indeed. Two losses so dear
Freed from trauma,
Freed from fear and prisons of so many.

I am boxed in; I see no way out.
I am boxed in; there might be a way out.

Months come and go.

I become freed and healed

Time marches on.

I am boxed in; I see no way out.

I am boxed in; I believe here's a way out.

From May to January hope knocks at the door

Once ignored; once neglected.

It says, "There's a plan that might be . . ."

I say, "If God's will it be, but not yet it be," and walked away.

It is commanded to stay and follow all my ways,

While shame and self-judgment are burned away.

I am boxed in; I see no way out.

I am boxed in; I believe there's a way out.

From May to January hope knocks at the door.

It says, "There's a plan that might be. . ."

I say, "if God's will it be, but not yet."

It stays and follows anyway. "Why," I say, "do you stay?"

I sense Christ is near and the gentle response;

"So you will come to know me all the more —

Christ your king."

I am boxed in; I see no way out.

I am boxed in; I believe there's a way out.

Day and night Hope declares,

"There's a plan that might be . . ."

I say, "I hear you, if God's will it be,

but not yet it be," and keep living.

I look to the sky and ask, "What's all this for?"

The gentle response comes and says, "Wait and see."

I am boxed in; I see no way out.

Hope declares, "There's a plan that might be. . ."

A lesson in sustainability and discipline rings bells,

Connects lessons of old made into habits of new.

These now go with attunement and validation.

No more shame and self-judgment.

Fortification is what goes with Hope.

Clarity's light turned on and shines on Romans 5: 2-5. [1]

I am boxed in; I see no way out.

I am boxed in; I wait for a way out.

Hope declares, "There's a plan that might be. . ."

I declare, "Christ, show me how to be more like you."

While others say, "Turn to Christ on bended knee,

---

[1] Through whom we have gained access by faith into this grace in which we now stand. And we boast in the hope of the glory of God. Not only so, but we also glory in our sufferings, because we know that suffering produces perseverance; perseverance, character, character, hope. And hope does not put us to shame, because God's love has been poured out into our hearts through the Holy Spirit, who has been given to us.

Who shows the way to liberty."

They say what I already know.

Bless their heart for they care so.

I pray for humility and wisdom, praying they come.

This way I may respond with a gentle and kind answer.

I am boxed in; I see no way out.

I am boxed in; Christ is worth more than a way out.

Life goes at a steady pace.

Hope still declares, "There's a plan that might be . . ."

I declare, "If God's will it be, for God's glory is worth far

More than the outcome of what might be."

I am boxed in; I see no way out.

I am boxed in; Christ is worth more than a way out.

I am tired and exhausted,

but I overcome the wall of fear set before me.

Hope declares, "There's a plan that might be . . ."

I say, "Hee yaw!" [2] and keep moving.

I am boxed in; I see no way out.

I am boxed in; Jesus is worth more than a way out.

I am tired; I am beat with one more lap to go.

I know Christ is guiding my feet.

---

[2] Steve Curtis Chapman)

I will finish; pray I finish strong.

Hope declares, "There's a plan that might be . . ."

Now I declare, "I have won my prize!

My hope restored and my joy complete in Christ my King."

I am boxed in; I see no way out.

I am boxed in; but oh wait,

Finally there's a way out.

I am no longer the person I was.

A path that was long and hard,

but throughout one could see God's grace.

This race is won at last and was finished well (Lord's will it
be).

I see a way out; the One guiding my feet.

It was Christ all along with his mercy and grace.

My name is Shayna; I live in Michigan with my lovable family of my parents, brother and sister (in-law). Plus, my three adopted sisters (how you are loved). I have a wonderful Christ centered, amazing church family and my friends. I enjoy biking, reading, doing crafts and hanging out with friends and family. To Laurel Plimpton my dear friend and editor (and including everyone listed above.) Thanks for your prayers and support; this was a team effort to get this here.

Thank you Jesus for being the Lord of my life; he defines who I am.

To you reader, thanks for taking time to read this. I pray you found this encouraging and helpful; directing your steps ever closer to our dear Savior and Lord. Blessings!

The God Who Whispers

Diane Furlong

"Shhh . . . I have something to tell you."

If those words were spoken in a whisper by a trusted friend, what would you do? Most likely you would stop, turn aside, and listen.

There's something special about a message that is whispered.

A whispered message is important. One does not use a whisper to tell the weather forecast - or the dinner menu.

A whisper is personal. It conveys a special message meant for one person only.

A whisper is kind. Angry voices are often loud, but the tone of a whisper is gentle.

The Bible states that God spoke to Elijah in "a gentle whisper" (1 Kings 19:19).

Perhaps God desires to speak to you today. Is it possible that He has been whispering, but that His gentle whisper has been drowned out by the noise of our world?

In the Psalms, the Lord invites us to "be still and know that I am God" (Psalm 46:10).

Put aside all distractions. Wait. Listen.

God knows us perfectly and loves us unconditionally. He knows our secret worries, hopes, and dreams.

Open His Word, read what He has written. Ask Him for ears to hear the gentle whisper of a loving Father.

Perhaps He is whispering your name right now. Listen. He might be saying words like these.

"I have loved you with an everlasting love."

"I will never leave you nor forsake you."

"Fear not, for I am with you."

"My grace is sufficient for you."

"Nothing can separate you from the love of God."

God loves you more than you can imagine. Turn aside. Listen. A gentle whisper is awaiting you.

Diane Furlong is retired and is living in Bradenton, Florida. She worked as a middle school teacher and as an occupational therapist. In retirement, she hopes to finally have time for writing.

Keeping the Heart Safe

Vicki Johnson

"Your word I have treasured in my heart,
That I may not sin against You."
Psalm 119:11

Mom's recent diagnosis of Alzheimer's was evident in every room of the house. A life-threatening illness had put her in the hospital, bringing me on a 1,000-mile trip back to my childhood home. My mission—find an elusive safe, which held important papers for my brother and me; the proverbial needle in a haystack.

In the few months since my last visit, Mom's pack-rat tendencies had overtaken every inch of living space, making it difficult to move without bumping into memory jogging castoffs.

As I surveyed the kitchen, unwanted recollections surfaced, bringing with them unwelcomed emotions. My jaw clenched as past hurts and bitterness, my feelings of inadequacy, her failure to be the mother I wanted, and a host of other foul responses simmered within me.

The longer I hunted through the sea of random throwaways, the more easily my harbored resentments broke loose from their sloppy moorings and maneuvered to the forefront of my thoughts.

I paused, swallowed deep, and prayed, *Please God, help me! I thought I had moved past these ancient emotions. We may not be close, but I do love my mom. I hate these ugly memories I battle when I'm here. How is it possible to have two opposite feelings for someone? I don't want to be this way. Please clear away the emotional debris. Help me to focus on You and the task I need to complete.*

I am with you, Daughter.

A verse came to mind from Joshua 1:9, "Have I not commanded you? Be strong and courageous! Do not tremble or be dismayed, for the LORD your God is with you wherever you go" (NASB).

Thank you, Lord. Amen, I whispered.

Mom's storehouse of prized possessions seemed to be her bedroom. Price-tagged, twenty-year-old outfits filled her closet. Brand new costume jewelry, stashed in a pair of sweatpants, were hidden in a clothes hamper. Odd assortments of "collectible" coins were stockpiled under her bed. Piles of previous Christmas and birthday gifts, still boxed, cluttered the floor.

Lord, why did she hold onto all this stuff? Why didn't she let go of these things instead of hoarding them?

A faint memory of Philippians 4:13 echoed in my mind, "I can do all things through Him who strengthens me" (NASB). Yes, Lord. Help me do all the things that are now mine to do, in Your strength.

It took almost a week to dismantle the mounds of odds and ends Mom had amassed before the safe was finally discovered. Elation changed to surprise and then dismay when my brother forced the safe open. In it was a curious mix of personal papers in yellowed envelopes, none of which we were looking for. My brother opened a yellowed letter from 1965, when I was 3 years old, and silently read the contents. He then handed it to me saying, "Do whatever you want with it."

I took it apprehensively and read. It was a scathing letter to my mother from "a concerned neighbor." This anonymous author railed against our family, and me in particular. Anger and disgust gripped my heart. What kind of person would write such a poison pen letter? What was the point?

Oh, Mom! You saved that vile thing, after all these years! What in the world made you keep it in your safe? Storing up bitterness and regret only results in a prison you keep yourself in. I release the hold this cruel message has held over you and all of us these past years.

My decision was quick and irrevocable. Into the shredder it went.

Then I sensed the Lord asking me that same question. *"Daughter, why is your heart safe-keeping the hurt from years past? Surrender your burden to me and let your heart be a treasure house of My Word."*

His words pricked my heart, but I knew it was for my good. Condemnation pains the heart, leaving us with no hope for restoration. Conviction pains the heart, pointing us to confession and the promise of full restoration in Christ.

Forgive me, Lord! Help me to forgive my mom for not being the person I needed her to be. Help me to be thankful for what she got right. Let the healing begin.

It's so easy to hold on to hurts and disappointments. We give them free room and board, even offering to check in on them to make sure they're doing okay. Left unchecked, they soon embed bitterness into everything we do.

God didn't design our hearts to store up grievances and pain, as real as they may be. His beautiful plan is that by His Grace our hearts and minds would release the hurt to Him. In exchange, we can treasure up His living Word, drawing from it daily and drinking deeply from its life-giving Truth.

In our blessing we are then able to bless others with the same whisper of Grace that sets the captive free.

You, my friend, are precious to God. He loves you with an everlasting Love.

If you are burdened by something from your past, tell the Lord what's on your heart. Cast your cares upon Him, for He cares for you. Ask Him to forgive you for holding onto that sin (the grievance) that has kept you separated from His Presence. Get into God's Word so God's Word can get into you. Try starting with Psalm 51 and 139.

Keep your heart safe in Jesus.

Vicki is a Midwest transplant in southeastern Pennsylvania. She has been married thirty-seven years to her pastor hubby with five grown children, three daughters-in-law, and five grandchildren. As a radio host at 1075AliveFM/WBYN, she signs off with 1 Thessalonians 5:24 "Faithful is He who calls you, and He will bring it to pass."

The Spirit Within

Misty Cramer

"The Spirit of God has made me, And the breath of the Almighty gives me life" Job 33:4 NIV.

As we walked into the nursing home, the pungent smells smacked us in the face. The aroma of the noon meal in combination with cleaning solution was anything but pleasant. Nevertheless, as we made our way through the entry area, we smiled and said hello to the residents who looked up from their wheelchairs, hungry for more than the lunch sitting before them.

"Hi, Grandpa!" we said as we walked into his room. He scooted himself up in his bed, smiled, and returned the greeting, always happy to see his grandchildren.

As the conversation began between our family, I glanced around the room. The cement walls provided no warmth or comfort, even with the scattered pictures taped on them by the resident's families. My mind wandered as I thought about what the lives of these men may have held. It was as if stories of adventure, laughter, heartache, love, and loss were locked up inside bodies that could no longer share with us all that the prior years had held. I wondered if there were beautiful love stories hidden in their hearts. Or perhaps some had fought in the war, and I was sitting in their room, living in the freedom I often took for granted because of their sacrifice. Maybe they had great adventures of vacations with their families at a nearby lake or a distant mountain range. I bet they sat at the head of the table during a large family gathering, proud of the children and grandchildren who surrounded them. Or maybe they were lonely. Maybe they didn't have a family at all, and they were living their last days in the same manner the years before them had been.

My thoughts were suddenly jolted by a gargled, yet loud, sound from one of the men in the bed behind me. As I shifted in my chair and looked, I smiled at a lady in the chair next to him. Her tiny body sat close to the bed, her hand stretched across the blanket, holding his hand. As the nurse made her way past me, she whispered in my ear, "His wife comes every day and sits with him, even though he never opens his eyes or talks."

Her statement spoke volumes, and I dismissed myself from Grandpa's bedside and pulled up a chair next to the woman. Above her husband's bed hung a small cross, surrounded by some family photos. I began to talk to the woman, and listened to her as she confirmed what the nurse had said. His unintelligible moans were frequent, coming several times each minute. From the reactions of his roommates and others who went in and out of the room, it was apparent the moaning had become as normal as the sounds of the nurses' chatter in the hallway.

It was after his wife shared about their family and her daily visits to sit with her husband that she disclosed the words that would forever be embedded into my heart. It was as if she was waiting to save the best for last. Perhaps adding an exclamation point to the end of a sentence.

"I don't even know if my husband knows I'm here. He moans loudly, around the clock. He doesn't speak . . . except for this. Whenever I sing 'Jesus Loves Me,' he joins right in and sings every word with me."

This frail body. This person who needed to be tended to for even the slightest needs. This man whose moans filled the room all day, every day. This man . . . this man would join his wife in singing "Jesus Loves Me" without missing a word.

I left the nursing home that day in awe of the love and commitment of a woman to her husband. A woman whose love was obvious as she displayed evidence of the words, "in sickness and in health . . . til death do us part." And I left with the Holy Spirit washing over me, filling me with the peace of knowing that even in our darkest times, even when it seems we can't be reached, even when life seems to have gone on without us, He is still present. His love and His promises reach into the darkness, take hold of us, drawing us deeper into His presence, and reminding us that He was there all the while.

Heavenly Father, I thank You for reaching me in the midst of my most difficult times. I praise You for touching my spirit, reminding me of Your presence during those times when I am fearful and restless, unsure of what the future holds. Amen

As a woman who has seen the story of redemption written throughout the chapters of her life, Misty uses her writing and speaking to point people to her Redeemer, Jesus. She and her husband of thirty-six years have five sons, two daughters-in-law, two adorable granddaughters, and reside in Michigan.

His Presence

Pam Lyons

You know how many times I've sat teary-eyed,
wanting for You to sit down, right next to me.
I've pleaded for You to take my hand,
to soothe me with the sound of Your voice.
Now it strikes me silly, even foolish,
that I longed for such encounters.

The fact is,
in this world, You, God,
never sit an arm's length away.
Instead, Your closeness dwells inside me,
nearer to my heart than any physical contact.
You warm my soul deeper than a well-placed hand,
And Your comfort is surer than a temporary hug.

You are here, willing to mend my deepest wounds.
Your faithfulness and mercy are unending,
and Your grace is my soul's eleventh-hour reprieve.

My spirit is prostrate before You, Lord,

as I meditate on the adoring love that burns here in me;

Your spirit dwelling within me, forever and ever.

Pam Lyons is a gifted Bible teacher, retreat speaker and facilitator. Her passion is to share scripture in an authentic and relevant way to deepen women's love for Christ. After serving ten years as the Director of LIFT, she remains active on several boards and attends Phoenix Seminary.

Little Graces Whispered by Our Big God

Rev. Jennifer E. Sakata

Grace is for the big stuff, or so we often think. Like when David committed adultery with Bathsheba and tried to cover it up. Or like when Moses, who was festering in anger and frustration, then lost his footing into the Promised Land because he *struck* the rock for water when God had said that a *word* to the rock directed by Him would do. Consider the famed woman at the well—a woman whose thirst for significance and meaning was met by a Savior whose bucket would never run dry and whose life cut through the substance of hers to a brand new one. Or among the most notable, think of the Apostle Paul and his power position, as he sought out and oversaw the deaths of any Christian in his path. For each of them, God's grace was life-sized, and its need was obvious. Big Grace.

One morning not long ago, grace came differently. More like a whisper, a gentle nudge, a "little" grace, that caught my attention. Some mornings, I come downstairs to the not-so-angelic choir of competing, comparing, and complaining, lived out in the voices and bodies of our two sons. They love Jesus, but like all of us who do, they, too, are much in need of grace and the continual filling only God and His Holy Spirit can bring. On a good day, I can hear those "conversations" as God's invitation to grow through conflict, trusting He put us together on purpose and is daily working out that purpose through His grace. On the not so good days . . . well, it's a melody I'm none too fond of, and find myself much in need of God's intervention to tune it out until I can receive His help to tune His grace in.

On this particular morning, I heard the sound of humming. First one son, then the other. Not sure I've ever heard a humming duet before, and definitely not coming from our boys at breakfast. But the sound was clear and the tune recognizable, as together their humming swelled and receded in all the right places. It was a song we had sung in worship and heard on the radio. "In Christ Alone" by Keith Getty and Stuart Townend, and they were humming it out, together.

In place of the chaos that is sometimes the start to our morning, God lifted me on the wings of grace through the gentle sounds of two kids in the kitchen having breakfast. And it changed the trajectory of our day. Whispering Grace.

Again and again, Scripture affirms the place and work of grace for any who would follow Jesus. When Elijah needed encouragement from God, it didn't come in the strength of the wind or the power of the earthquake or even in the force of the fire. God's word of help and redirection came to Elijah in a gentle whisper. "What are you doing here Elijah? . . . Go back the same way you came . . . *I will yet preserve 7000 others in Israel . . . "* (1 Kings 19: 13-18, NLT). Fast forward to a quiet conversation between two friends on a beach in Galilee. "Peter, son of John, do you love me more than these?" (John 21: 15-19). A whisper of a question, right in the middle of an ordinary day, after eating an ordinary meal . . . three-times repeated, each with the invitation to let God's grace do its best work: forgiven, freed, and moving forward.

No matter the size of the sin, regardless of the extent of the infraction, grace names sin for what it is, and leaves in its place release and restoration. In the midst of our ordinary, run-of-the-mill daily sins, God's whispering grace reaches toward us and digs into us. We don't deserve it; we don't earn it. But out of God's incredible generosity, grace leaves its beauty mark all over the lives of those who will receive it and live into the freedom that God alone grants.

Sometimes, it's in the *giving* of grace, releasing others in response to God's Grace having been released to us first. Proverbs 17: 9 reminds us, "Love prospers when a fault is forgiven, but dwelling on it separates close friends" (NLT). Whispers of "little" graces are given permission to do their unbinding work when we choose to look past another's annoying habits. Or when we choose to keep silent about someone's clear weakness, acknowledging it took a lifetime for those fractures to develop, while trusting God's grace works best in weakness (2 Corinthians 12:9). Grace is whispered when we look past a word carelessly spoken. Or a commitment too easily forgotten. "Little" graces are whispered when we turn our eyes more regularly to the One who loved us first, rather than on the list of shortcomings of the ones God's given us to love in the now, whether in our home or our neighborhood or our work, or even in God's church. Whispering Grace.

At other times, it's in the humble *receiving* of such whispered graces we find our freedom and remember our place at God's Big-Enough Table. We see all too clearly our own cracks and brokenness. A harsh thought here, an unfiltered word there. A schedule too jam-packed for patience, and commitments too numerous for unplanned 'interruptions.' And then there in the midst of it all we receive an email reminding us Whose we are. Or a text that someone's been praying. Our Bible falls open to 'just the right scripture.' A friend asks to go on a walk. Or, we hear the sound of humming in the kitchen. Little Graces whispered by our Big God.

Much as we need God's *big* grace, that initial place of forgiving us and ushering us into our relationship with Him, I am learning to be attentive to these every day "little" graces. It's these heaven-sent whispers that ultimately sustain and reorient us in our ordinary every day. Grace is meant to capture our attention, and turn us toward God once again.

Sometimes God's grace is big and moves mountains. Other times, God's grace whispers . . . and sometimes, God's grace even hums in the kitchen.

Jennifer Sakata lives in Washington, IL with husband Craig, and sons Ethan and Seth. Jennifer believes in date nights with your husband, game nights with your kids and backyard barbecues with your neighbors. You might also catch her cycling on her pink-tired road bike hollering hello to anyone who'll wave.

Worship in the Wasteland

Debbie D. Daniel

Smoke from the fire blackens the sky.
Birds that once circled no longer fly.
Surveying the scarred earth, I start to cry,
How is it that somehow I did not die?

This was the home of my little nest.
This was the place where I could find rest.
Years I spent building and working away.
Gone. It's all gone, in less than a day.

Gone, too, the memories, the laughter, the dreams,
Years spent on them were wasted, it seems.
For now there is nothing but ashes and tears.
What will be spent on the rest of my years?

My tears blend with ashes and form a thick clay.
I stare, my body beginning to sway.
More tears, more mud – I can't move around.
I cry out in hopes that I will be found.

But part of me hopes that no hero will come.
The pain is too much, and my spirit is numb.
Perhaps I should stay, let go, and sink in.
Oh! To not face what was lost again!

To not feel the sting of words hurled at me,
To not view the grief on the faces I see,
To not miss the one who no longer is near,
To not feel that there is no reason I'm here.

I silence my cry and stand still in the mire,
Amazed that I did fall victim to fire.
There is no way this could happen to me.
This is not how I thought it would be.

My body, my heart, my voice are all still.
Will I become the fire's last kill?
Or will I once again find I can stand?
Find my voice, find hope, find the future You've planned?

You saved me already from consuming fire,
Now rescue me from this deepening mire.
Set my feet on a rock and help me to stand
Deliver me, please, from this ravaged land.

Turn my groanings and cries to praises and song,
Redeem, restore, make right what went wrong.
But even if not, if all must stay lost,
I'll sing still to you still, no matter the cost.

For lands and nests and temporal things
Are not the reason my spirit still sings.
That's all just muck and mire and clay
That doesn't last. It all goes away.

The reason my spirit can still sing and praise
Will always be You, and Your gracious ways.
May others witness the song that I raise,
And trust You, too, for all of their days.

Psalm 40:1-3

"I waited patiently for the Lord;
he turned to me and heard my cry.
He lifted me out of the slimy pit,
Out of the mud and mire;
He set my feet on a rock
And gave me a firm place to stand.
He put a new song in my mouth,
A hymn of praise to our God.
Many will see and fear the Lord
And put their trust in him."

Debbie Daniel is a divorced mom of three. She lives in Florida with her children, ages seven, sixteen, and twenty. She loves Jesus, her kids, and words.

Trusting in God's Grace

Rosemary Sandefer

My oldest son's teen years were miserable. When Troy was twelve, his father and I were divorced. Not knowing that his father planned to marry soon after the divorce, he chose to stay and be company for his dad. Disappointed that his father wasn't giving him much attention, he began smoking marijuana, drinking beer, and living a life that called for a lot of prayer from mom. I prayed that someone would come into his life who would lead him to Jesus, and I prayed that for him during all of his life.

After he turned nineteen, Troy moved to Florida and we saw him occasionally. He had a sensitive and giving heart, and often chose women friends who were in need. He married and divorced twice. He became an alcoholic and used drugs. Despite his destructive habits, he was a talented carpenter and built many beautiful homes. Eventually, in his fifties, his rough living took its toll and he lost friends, his beautiful home and his livelihood. A friend who owned apartments allowed him to live in one of them in exchange for doing needed renovations.

In October of 2017 we met at a restaurant to celebrate his 57th birthday. He looked very thin and complained that he had a lot of pain from lifting a heavy door. In November, we joined him for Thanksgiving dinner at his favorite restaurant. He seemed very quiet and didn't eat much. His back was still hurting. The next week, his sister, Chris, called a couple of times to ask if I'd talked to Troy. The second time, she shared with me that he was "supposed to" tell mom that his back problem turned out to be a large tumor in his lung. It was pressing on his heart -- it was inoperable because of its location. In that call I learned my first-born son was dying.

My husband and I retired to Florida in 2008 and lived about an hour away from Troy. We quickly turned our porch into a bedroom for him. Chris and her husband were vacationing in Florida, but changed their plans and helped us care for Troy those last six weeks of his life. His brother and another sister flew from Michigan to Florida to move him out of his apartment and into our home. We welcomed hospice care into our home in mid-January of 2018.

During this same time my husband and I were struggling through numerous challenges. Just before we moved Troy into our home, I had a stroke that affected my peripheral vision leaving me unable to drive. My husband's bad knee put him in pain, on crutches, unable to work and needing a knee replacement which was scheduled for March. Our sister-in-law died mid-February after a long struggle with Parkinson's. Through all of this we were comforted and covered in prayer by our pastors, church elders, close friends and relatives.

Chris and I prayed for Troy constantly, hoping he would come to know the Lord. During that time, Chris, a devoted lover of Jesus, had an opportunity to talk with him about heaven. Troy asked "How far do we go up?" A little surprised by the question, she answered, "You go up 'til you see the light."

Our pastor came to see Troy, but he was ordered out of the bedroom. Troy was very defiant when the subject of faith came up—except with Chris. Chris and I had a strong feeling that Satan was actively seeking his soul. We found a CD of hymns with Jesus' name in all of the songs, and we played it in his room as much as we could. We laid hands on him and prayed over him often.

On February 28, 2018, we went to bed knowing that this was probably the last night Troy would be with us on this earth. As I went to bed, I prayed, "Father, you have promised that my son would be saved, but there isn't much time. I don't know how it will happen, but please have mercy on his soul." About 2 a.m. the hospice nurse woke us to say that he had died. Her words were "He had a very peaceful death. He opened his eyes very wide, looked up, got a smile on his face, and took his last breath."

Was this a sign? Did he look up and see "the light?"

After Troy passed we had strong confirmations that Satan's efforts to win his soul were foiled.

Our daughter had been at a Bible study the weekend before Troy's death. They prayed for us and for Troy's salvation. On the way out, the leader stopped everyone and said. "We need to stop right now and pray for Troy, Satan is attacking him."

Another daughter's Bible study group was praying for Troy's salvation too, and they assured her that their prayers would be heard. "But how will we know," she asked. "There will be a sign," they responded.

The third confirmation came from our pastor. I called him after Troy's death and shared with him our suspicions that Satan had been after Troy's soul. He was not surprised. The evening after he tried to visit and pray with Troy, he was with friends, recounting his experience. One of those friends shared his strong feeling that Satan was fighting for Troy's soul, and that they needed to pray against this satanic attack.

It was our faith, hope in God's mercy, and the love that flowed to us from Jesus, our children, grandchildren, relatives and friends, that encouraged and comforted us through this challenge. I believe it was in God's plan to bring Troy to our home, to have his sister Chris with him, and to have many prayer warriors storming heaven for God's mercy.

Was it the light of heaven Troy saw that made him smile? Was that the promised sign— a sign of God's grace? My heart says "YES!"

Rosemary Sandefer lives in Lady Lake, Florida, with her husband Jim. They share seven children, nineteen grandchildren, and twelve great-grandchildren. She credits God for giving her the inspiration to found Shared Pregnancy Women's Center in Lansing, Michigan, which in 2020 celebrated its 38th year of serving women and families with unexpected and/or problem pregnancies.

My Father's Canvas

Laura D. Garry

Dead less than a week, he still managed to turn my life upside down. Steadying myself in the exact place the police officers discovered his body, my tear-filled eyes scanned the unfamiliar room. I doubted anyone from the coroner's office noticed his paintings, but each one attracted my immediate attention. Recreations of his favorite painter, Johannes Vermeer, an untrained eye might be fooled. I saw how he half-heartedly propped each painting upon his worn-out Victorian furniture, rather than securing his work tight to the room's bright pink walls. Anything but elegant, the olive-green couch sat lopsided. The mahogany base bowed under the weight of several antique frames. *Girl with a Pearl Earring* stood out to me more than any of the other pieces of his art. Grasping my surroundings, I realized his living area doubled as the check-in area for the small motel he ran. The sole picture nailed to the wall, a photograph of him snapped during an award ceremony, hung sideways. My gaze caught his. *What color were Dad's eyes?* I should know. Instead, all I recalled were eyes that rarely greeted mine.

I didn't want to face the mess in front of me. The clutter of Dad's unkempt house echoed the chaos of his life. There was not a will that I knew of, just a recent divorce. Earlier that year, I received a handwritten note from wife number three, describing his multiple affairs. Thirteen years before her flowered pink envelope arrived in my mailbox, she, too, met my dad on the internet, a website geared for people aged fifty and older. He was still married to wife number two at the time. I grabbed an empty packing box and headed for Dad's desk, in front of the window facing the motel parking lot. The well-worn chair at the desk held a faded and ripped seat cushion deeply imprinted from hours of noticeable wear. I pictured Dad spending his days gazing out the window, past the parking lot, to the main street of the small Minnesota town.

As I removed the first pieces of paper scattered on the desk, I discovered the motel check-in book. Even after all this time, I recognized Dad's handwriting. Many years ago, after his first wife—my mother—left, I spent time copying his name over and over to forge absentee slips for when I skipped school. At the time, I was glad he went by his middle name, Bruce, rather than his first name. His B was easy to reproduce because it was a straight line with two triangles forming the letter. He did the same thing with his P, the first letter of our last name.

I stared at the ledger. There were only names listed. No addresses. No phone numbers. Nothing. Everything in pencil, barely legible. It was how life had always been with Dad—indecipherable. No details. No responsiveness. Alive, he remained distant. But now, in death, uncovering his dusty desk I slowly began to expose him. I heard his secrets start to whisper, but I plugged my ears and prayed, "God, please help me. May the whispers of Your grace be what I hear."

I did not come to know Christ until my early twenties. Experiencing a childhood with distant parents like mine, succumbing to shame became my frequent reality. As a child, I only knew to deem the distance of my parents as my fault. I grew up believing I must have said or done something to push my parents away. An example is the strange way I found out about Dad and his third wife. Most likely, I wouldn't have known, except that his second wife, Carol, insisted that he tell me. At the time, my husband, four kids, and I lived in an old home. We discovered bats in the attic after chasing several of them through our living room with a tennis racket in the dead of night. Trying to save some money, my husband and a couple of men from our church fastened themselves on the high-pointed roof. Sweating in the late Saturday morning sun, they did their best to pry loose layer upon layer of old, brittle shingles.

As they were struggling, the kids and I worked to make lunch. The phone rang while I was shredding a roast, and I answered without looking at the number. I stood, stunned, when I heard his voice, stopping my meal preparations to catch my breath. The jarring abruptness of his call was so reminiscent of life with Dad.

Why is he calling? I thought. *I haven't heard from him in months.*

"Laura, I am on my way to your house," I heard him say. "I should be there in about a half-hour or so. I am bringing someone with me."

Dad rarely visited us and had never dropped by on short notice. His words left me confused.

"Is Carol with you?" I asked.

"No. I am divorcing Carol. I am bringing my new girlfriend to meet you and the kids."

I wasn't sure what to say about his news, let alone the notion of him coming to introduce his new girlfriend to our kids. I doubted he would recall any of his grandchildren's names, and most likely, they wouldn't recognize their grandfather, either.

"New girlfriend?" I asked.

"Yes, see you soon." With that, he hung up.

I dropped the fork in my hand, and as it fell in the half-shredded beef, I ran out the back door of the house. I started yelling at the top of my lungs, which is problematic by the way, since I have a voice similar to Minnie Mouse.

"My Dad is coming! You need to come off the roof!" I knew my husband couldn't hear a word I was saying. "Now! Get down here! I need you to come off the roof!"

Even though he was high in the air, I could tell my husband was annoyed. As he descended the ladder, I waited to say anything more. His feet hit the grass, and as he turned toward me, my face communicated trouble even before I opened my mouth.

"My dad just called. He said he would be here in a half-hour with his new girlfriend."

Usually, my husband would be much more amusing in his response. In that instant, surprised as I was, he stayed quiet.

"Should we tell the guys to head home?" I asked.

My husband nodded and returned up the ladder to let the guys know they had the rest of the afternoon off.

Dad arrived as I finished putting lunch on the table. He and his new girlfriend came into our house, acting like teenagers. Hardly visiting at all, I don't think they stayed thirty minutes. Dad didn't even ask to see his grandchildren, who were playing in the yard. The visit, all about him, reminded me why our relationship stayed awkward and challenging.

All these years later, sorting through Dad's papers, I found myself also sorting memories. Most moments with Dad were unreadable like his check-in register, yet in reflection, this one stood out. How I wished my dad knew the unconditional love of God. Of course, I cannot fully understand Dad's experience, but his parents, distant too, left him alone. Desperate for love, he turned to women to fill the void. When he became a parent, he raised me the way his parents raised him.

After I became a Christian in my early twenties, I mistakenly believed God would instantaneously heal my family's hurt. Now in my forties, it had taken years of Bible study and prayer to accept my identity as God's daughter. Just as the men on the roof of our house did their best to pry loose layers of old, brittle shingles, generations of family dysfunction need prying off one layer at a time. The healing process moved slow.

I looked deep into *Girl with a Pearl Earring*, who peered at me from her home atop Dad's couch. I would be lying if I said comparing the time Dad spent with her to the hours he spent with me did not hurt. As his only daughter, I wish he had been receptive to mending our relationship. In the end, Dad died alone in this room. Motel guests dialed 9-1-1 when they found him unresponsive on the floor.

Sobbing, I looked down. "Dad, I am so sorry you died here alone. I wish I could have told you I love you one last time." I finally knew what I needed: "Dad, I know you never meant to hurt me. I forgive you." Standing in the place where Dad died, my eyes turned back to his painting. "God, at this moment, I understand. *Girl with a Pearl Earring* was Dad's canvas, but I am Yours. Your love is slowly changing me closer to the resemblance of Your Son."

Laura believes life change in Christ is possible as one wrestles with the whys of thoughts, feelings, and actions. A devotional writer with a master's degree in theological studies from the University of Northwestern in St. Paul, Minnesota, Laura helps readers wrestle out their whys through Scripture. Connect at www.lauradgarry.com.

Your Wild Card

Colette Schaffer

Don't you love when a verse of scripture that you have read, seemingly a thousand times, grabs your attention to teach you a little more? I was reading out of 2 Corinthians 12 when verse 9 spoke a little clearer to my heart. It reads, "'My grace is sufficient for you, for My strength is made perfect in weakness.'"

Not Enough

As humans, we fall short of being good enough, or strong enough, or even smart enough. The list of not being enough is an extensive one. We know we need Jesus to bridge the gap for our salvation, but what about the rest of the potholes in our lives? 2 Corinthians 12:9 isn't talking about when we get to Heaven. We are not going to have weaknesses when we get there—praise God! No, we are weak now and need His grace to fill in the potholes in our lives every moment. It is when we have come to the end of our own abilities, our own strength, our own knowledge, our own words, and our own energy when we can see God move if we let Him.

☐I was raised in a Christian home. I have loved reading the Bible from a young age—I even teethed on a little pink New Testament. However, there was one famous passage of scripture that never seemed to make sense to me. The scripture passage is most commonly known in the gospels as the beatitudes that Jesus preached in His famous "Sermon on the Mount" (Matthew 5:3-12).

Divine Assistance

The Beatitudes is a beautiful passage of scripture, but I was always confused thinking Jesus was saying that it was a good thing to be poor in spirit, or sad, or to be hungry . . . that doesn't sound good to me, I know that God is good. So, what then does it mean? As I researched this passage of scripture, I found that the word "Blessed" here is another word for grace. \

Merriam-Webster's dictionary defines grace as "unmerited divine assistance given to humans," or "a special favor." It also means to have "divine assistance." I like that! I don't know about you, but I could use some divine assistance more times than not. Therefore, if you plug that definition in for blessed, it means that although you may be facing a tough situation, you have God's assistance available to help you make up the difference you lack. He will strengthen you when your own strength isn't enough. He will give you wisdom when you don't know what to do. He will restore peace to you when your world has been shaken.

Pull Your Wild Card

Grace is like your 'wild card.' Have you ever been playing cards and had a terrible hand? It might have looked as though the game was over for you, then by pure luck, you drew a wild card. That card made up for what you were lacking and turned the game around for you, if not helping you win. Grace is just like that wild card—it is what you need to be successful in this crazy game of life. No matter what other proverbial cards you are holding, grace completes what you lack to succeed.

So, how do you draw the 'wild card' of grace in your life? Acknowledge God in every situation. Proverbs 3:5-6 says, "Trust in the Lord with all your heart, and lean not on your own understanding; In all your ways acknowledge Him, and He will direct your paths." □Matthew 6:33 also talks about seeking Him first, and everything you are lacking (are in need of) will be added to you.

Seek God First

Trust God with everything in your life. I don't believe that you should have a list of ranking priorities like God first, your spouse second, kids third, etc. Instead, you should seek God first in your marriage, seek Him as a parent, in your job, clear down the line to your hobbies. When you seek Him first, He will give you His grace - His blessing, in that area. Don't wait to seek Him till you come to the end of yourself and your abilities. You will waste a lot of time and energy trying to do things your own way. No, acknowledge that His ways and thoughts are higher than yours (Isaiah 55:9). Seek Him (draw that wild card of grace), and you will win every time.

Jeremiah 29:11 says, "For I know the thoughts that I think toward you, says the Lord, thoughts of peace and not of evil, to give you a future and a hope." Most of us can probably quote this verse, but do you know what verses 12-14 go on to say? The scripture says that YOU have a part to play. Your role is to seek Him, call on Him, and pray to Him. When you act on that Word, He can and will fulfill His promise to strengthen you in your weakness and bring you peace. He will make up the difference in what you are lacking. His grace, is in fact, sufficient for you. He will hand you the wild card of grace to make you complete and successful in all you do.

Colette Schaffer is known for her down-to-earth, straight-talking style of preaching and teaching the Word. She is author of *Planted: A Guided Study to Produce a Peace-Filled Life in an Anxiety-Filled World and Expecting Jesus: An Advent Devotional.* Colette also shares weekly insights on her blog at schafferministries.com.

Turn Toward the Son

Heather Stamper

"Let me hear Your lovingkindness in the morning; For I trust in You; Teach me the way in which I should walk; For to You I lift up my soul. Deliver me, O Lord, from my enemies; I take refuge in You. Teach me to do Your will, For You are my God; Let Your good Spirit lead me on level ground."
Psalm 143:8-10 (NASB)

This morning while driving, I noticed one yard in my neighborhood was dotted with clusters of buttercups. The simple yellow flowers caught my eye as I drove by admiring their full blooms. The most remarkable thing was that all the flowers were facing in one direction. I remember learning years ago that plants would grow in the direction of the sun to absorb its energy for maximum growth. This was more than that; all their little flower faces were opened and aimed directly toward the sun. It was as if they were tiny satellite dishes that had all been tuned and targeted for the same exact coordinates, and they were locked in to receive the sunshine and all it had to offer. The Lord stirred a message from deep within: "All creation worships Me. Even the tiny flowers know to turn their gaze on Me first thing in the morning. They will be recharged, restored and given energy from My sun for today. So, too, should you turn to My Son in the morning. I will recharge, restore and give you energy."

Father God, thank You for every new day. I see Your perfection in creation, and my heart answers back, "Yes! As the flowers turn their faces to you, so shall I turn my face and be open to receive You. Amen."

Heather Stamper lives with her husband, their two boys, and their dog in Texas. She unashamedly sings and dances in her kitchen while she cooks, plays silly games with her kids, and is passionate about ministries to develop friendships where people can laugh together, learn together, and live intentionally together.

Strength and Grace

Leann Seale

*"Three times I pleaded with the Lord to take it away from me.
But he said to me, "My grace is sufficient for you, for my power is
made perfect in weakness." Therefore I will boast all the more
gladly about my weaknesses, so that Christ's power may rest on
me."*
2 Corinthians 12:8-9

When we are in a crisis, our world stops as we know it. Things change and priorities shift. We go into survival mode, and during these times, God does his finest work. We learn far more about ourselves and the faithfulness of God when we are in the middle of a storm than when the waters are calm. We learn to rely on God to sustain us. For when we are weak, He reveals His strength.

In 2017, I went in for a routine mammogram. A second mammogram and a biopsy later, I learned I had breast cancer.

When I heard those words, I was in shock and disbelief. On the drive home from the doctor, the Scripture from James 1:2-4 played over and over in my head, *"Consider it pure joy, my brothers and sisters, whenever you face trials of many kinds, because you know that the testing of your faith produces perseverance. Let perseverance finish its work so that you may be mature and complete, not lacking anything."*

I knew I was about to set out on a path that was going to be rough, but I also had a spark deep inside of pure joy — because God has ALWAYS been faithful. He brought good out of difficult seasons in the past, and I knew God had never left me alone before. Surely, He wouldn't start now.

I never would have chosen to have cancer. My life will forever be altered because of it. And, gratefully, I am cancer free now although I live with daily bone pain and some hearing loss from chemo. Additionally, there are scars from surgeries, medicine to take, and fears that linger. Yet, suffering and trials allowed me to see God up close, to become secure in His faithfulness and blessed by His grace. God works through pain in each of our lives to bring joy and blessings even in suffering. For that reason, I would never trade this experience.

Blessings came as friends rallied by my side: praying, bringing meals, helping in tangible ways, or sending cards and texts. After 29 years of wonderful marriage, my husband and I grew even stronger, more tender and more compassionate than ever. He loved me well, attending all twelve rounds of chemo, every doctor appointment and surgery, and caring for me through it all.

I had asked one thing of God before going into chemo — if He would not remove this cup, then please be my strength and grace each day. "Strength and grace" became my mantra. He provided these gifts faithfully like manna, just enough for one day. I needed to ask and rely on Him again for the next day, and He did not disappoint.

When making decisions, I prayed and relied on God for peace, and He gave it. When I should have been afraid going into surgery, I felt peace as I was carried by the prayers of my friends and family — buoyant though on a rough sea.

At times I felt overwhelmed and depleted. My relationship with the Lord and my investment in Bible study and worship gave me a storehouse of promises concerning God's character and goodness to draw from and get me through. Truth echoed in my heart and mind. It restored me. Praise God for the way He uses pain to grow our faith and trust. We are never the same, and I am grateful.

I am reminded of the C.S. Lewis quote from *The Problem of Pain*, "We can ignore even pleasure. But pain insists upon being attended to. God whispers to us in our pleasures, speaks in our conscience, but shouts in our pains: it is his megaphone to rouse a deaf world."

A year after my cancer treatment, my parents moved to Arizona. Days after the last box was unpacked, my parents were in the backyard when they heard two explosions that sounded like fireworks. Then the smell of fire. Instead of going through the side door of the garage, as he usually did, my dad went through the house to find the garage on fire. His usual route would have led to where the blast began. God's grace was already in motion.

The garage was a loss and the house suffered smoke and water damage throughout. Two faulty golf cart batteries had exploded, causing the destruction of Christmas decorations, tools my dad had inherited from his dad, and keepsakes from fifty years of marriage. That evening, neighbors gathered in the street, bringing food and water to my parents. In the days to follow, they were prayed for and cared for by these new neighbors. Though my parents were devastated and overwhelmed, they could see God's sovereignty and grace. They most importantly had each other. Their house has now been beautifully rebuilt with a sign from Isaiah 61:3: "Beauty from Ashes."

Trials grow our faith when we choose to trust God to be in control. He gives us peace and joy in the midst of suffering. Jesus said, "Peace I leave with you; my peace I give you. I do not give to you as the world gives. Do not let your hearts be troubled and do not be afraid" (John 14:27 NIV).

Suffering has purpose. God uses these times to show us a bigger picture, purpose, and plan. We come out refined, stronger, and more compassionate. So, dear friend, when faced with a trial, remember God is good. He is faithful.

Never will He leave you; never will He forsake you. He will be your strength and grace.

Leann Seale is a devoted wife, mother of four sons, a Bible study leader, MOPS mentor mom, and contributing devotional writer for her church. She is an energetic, down-to-earth speaker and writer who passionately shares life's lessons about marriage, family, and faith. Her blog can be found at LeannSeale.com

God Must Have Chuckled

Cheryl Ann Denton

Once upon a *true* time, there was a young girl called Annabelle. She imagined herself speaking to thousands and moving masses with the message of Jesus. She felt confident of her dream because she had prayed, "Lord, I'll go anywhere; I'll do anything You want."

Certainly, if she grew close enough, surrendered enough, and prayed enough, her destiny would be all that she dreamed.

Annabelle and her preacher-husband started their ministry at a Christian school in a small, southern community.

Population 227, small.

Being a city girl, it took her a while to enjoy collards, a local green delight, and to cook deer. When asked her future plans, she smiled and quoted her husband, "We'll only be here one, maybe two years."

God must have chuckled.

Three children later, Annabelle's restlessness magnified. *What's next, Lord?*

His response? "Don't be weary in well-doing: for in due season you will reap if you faint not" (Galatians 6:9).

Twelve years passed. Twelve long years. Many wonderful memories. Many wonderful people. But frustration and discontent often knocked on Annabelle's heart.

Surely, Lord, You have more for us? He said, "My grace is sufficient."

Finally, Annabelle and her husband accepted an invitation to teach at a Bible school in the former Soviet Union. Annabelle was delighted. She thought, *This is our big chance. We will finally have a bigger ministry.* (She has since repented of that attitude.)

God must have chuckled.

Annabelle's "big ministry" morphed into homeschooling *and* washing dishes and clothes in the bathtub. Her husband taught hundreds of future preachers while she spent hours preparing meals on a two-burner stove balanced precariously on a small table. Her household hurdles loomed larger than her kid's ministry on the street and her one Bible class.

How long would they minister overseas? They were willing to stay for a lifetime. However, after just four-and-a-half years, God surprised their family by sending them back to pastor in the small southern community where they began as newlyweds. Population now 201.

God must have chuckled.

He saw their twenty-plus year journey ahead with this same church family and community. He saw that Annabelle was thrilled with the move. How do I know?

My nickname is Annabelle, a fact known only by a few.

Also, known only by a few, is my inward journey. My outward journey may appear glamorous to some: writing, composing, directing dramas, preaching, teaching, and doing missions work. But my struggle was real when it came to learning contentment after God's path turned out different than I dreamed.

My desire was to be like Peter on the Day of Pentecost, but God's desire for me was to be like those in the shadows of the Upper Room. They also received a God assignment. Their stories did not make publication, but the lives they touched were just as valuable as the three thousand who heard Peter's sermon.

Now I realize God wasn't just chuckling about His plans for me, He was actually smiling. He paved my path with grace and helped me realize that the size of my platform didn't matter. Because of that realization, my husband and I didn't faint, and we reaped an amazing harvest. Our former students at the Christian school we lead have become our church deacons, musicians, department leaders, and teachers.

Just another reason for God to chuckle.

Cheryl Denton was born out west, married, and moved east, and has traveled the world in ministry with her husband, Buddy. She enjoys sharing Jesus through speaking, music, drama, and writing. Her three children, their spouses, and six grandchildren always widen her smile. More than anything, Cheryl loves, lov'n Jesus.

Masterpiece

Lisa C. Whitaker

It's early morning and I sit quietly on my front porch and watch as all of creation awakens from slumber. The sky loses its grip on darkness and in its place are the most beautiful shades of pink and orange. The colors deepen and become bolder as the sun reaches the horizon and then like the grand climax in a symphony, the sun bursts into view. The birds sing their praises, erupting in applause for the amazing display before them, and the wind gently sways the trees, keeping tempo. I close my eyes and I listen as all of creation sing to their Creator, each of them building in crescendo and then softening as if giving voice to another. How beautiful the sound. How beautiful the painting—the artwork that appears, as the music plays on. It's as if God has turned on the stereo in his art studio as He works on yet another masterpiece, and I get to sit quietly in the corner and watch it unfold. I get to watch the Master at work.

As I sit in my corner observing, Jesus begins to speak, my heart is listening. He reminds me of two things that concern his masterpieces. First, all his creation points to him. Romans 1:20 says, "For since the creation of the world God's invisible qualities—his eternal power and divine nature—have been clearly seen, being understood from what has been made, so that men are without excuse" (NIV). I look out, taking in the view around me, and I can see whispers of God's grace. It's in the movement of the trees as their branches reach toward heaven and sway gently with the wind. It's in the rising of the sun that brings light to a dark world. It's in the choir of birds singing songs of thanksgiving for another glorious morning. And it's in the beauty of a newly bloomed flower that has been given new life after the dead of winter.

Jesus speaks again to my heart, reminding me of the second thing regarding his masterpieces. He reminds me that I am one of His works of art. A masterpiece fashioned by His own hands. Ephesians 2:10 tells us, "For we are God's masterpiece. He has created us anew in Christ Jesus, so we can do the good things he planned for us long ago" (NLT). Psalm 139:13-16 says, "For you created my inmost being; you knit me together in my mother's womb. I praise you because I am fearfully and wonderfully made; your works are wonderful, I know that full well. My frame was not hidden from you when I was made in the secret place. When I was woven together in the depths of the earth, your eyes saw my unformed body. All the days ordained for me were written in your book before one of them came to be" (NIV).

As God speaks these truths, my heart joins with the rest of creation and sings at the realization that God sees me as a work of art—His masterpiece. My heart sings praises to the One who has shown me His grace through the works of His hand. Did you know that you, too, are a masterpiece of God? Is your heart singing today?

Lisa Whitaker is a writer and speaker. She is currently blogging at lisacwhitaker.com and shares her love of God on her Facebook ministry page, *Hold Fast Ministries*. Lisa is a Bible teacher for Women's Ministries at Liberty Bible Church in Chesterton, IN.

Of Grief and Grace

Mary Ellen Zent

"The Lord gave and the Lord has taken away, blessed be the name of the Lord."
Job 1:21b NASB

The first time we meet Job in the biblical book bearing his name, he had already lost all of his children, all his servants, all his oxen, all his donkeys, all his sheep, all his camels. He had lost everything he owned. I don't know about you, but if I were Job you probably wouldn't see me falling to the ground in worship, thanking God that He had given me all these riches to enjoy in the first place. No, I would likely be shouting at God, "It's not fair! Why are you taking all I have? I would be happy to give you SOME of my possessions, but why must you take ALL of them?

I was born with spina bifida, resulting in paralysis in my lower limbs among several other complications. Years ago, my doctor told me that spina bifida is not a progressive disability. Unlike muscular dystrophy (MD), multiple sclerosis (MS), or eye diseases like macular degeneration, the injuries resulting from spina bifida usually occur in the womb and do not worsen as the individual matures. However, my doctor neglected to warn me that as I grow older, the aging process itself would take a toll on my body. Well, it can, it did, and it does.

So, how does all of this connect? Well, when unexpected physical problems suddenly start to appear, what do I do? Do I respond in rebellion and throw a temper tantrum? Unfortunately, sometimes I do. But God is teaching me through the life of Job that He has not promised a life of ease without difficulties. Nor is He obligated to give me one without the other. He already pours out blessings on me every day. I only need to recognize those blessings for what they are. Sounds simple, doesn't it? Anyone can thank God for His bountiful gifts when current suffering is not a reality. But when He chooses to remove those generous gifts, and His shouts of love become faint whispers, I'm learning the truth of Job's benediction: "The Lord gave and the Lord has taken away. Blessed be the name of the Lord."

Born in November 1953, Mary Ellen Zent was not expected to live, but God planned otherwise! Her education includes a diploma from Long Ridge Writers Group and degrees from two other educational institutions. She is an avid reader and is currently enjoying some of the classics on her new Kindle.

Worship Whispers

Donna M. Fagerstrom

"Come let us bow down in worship, let us kneel before the Lord
our Maker; for He is our God and we are the people of
His pasture, the flock under His care."
Psalm 95:6-7

My earliest memories were surrounded by music. When my sister and I were five years old, a kind man came to our home with a delivery. He was from our small-town local music store. He knocked at the door, and to our surprise our eyes could hardly believe the sight of brand-new bright blue and shiny red accordions. My sister and I were beyond excited. I don't even remember who chose what color; the important thing was we were going to learn how to play the accordion. That hope was soon dashed when my dad came home from work. He was a very loving and kind man, but he knew we couldn't afford those musical instruments and the required lessons. They had to go back the next day. We cried. Mom cried.

As soon as my sister and I entered first grade, Mom went to work full-time so she could do the "extras" for the family, like private music lessons. Before long, a discerning adult told my mom that my sister and I had beautiful voices and we should take private voice lessons. At age ten, we started the lessons, which, for me, continued into married and ministry life. I had a song in my heart from my earliest memory. I recall my first voice teacher emphasizing, "Donna, pay careful attention to the lyrics of the song you sing. If they are not true in your own life, you are singing a lie." I have never forgotten her wise words. To this day, if the lyrics are not true in my own life, the song doesn't get sung. Worship is about Him, not me.

When my husband and I were newly married, we accepted a pastoral position of youth and music at a church in Colorado. The term "worship" wasn't the significant word it is today. However, personal worship was exactly what I learned to do as a result of living in the Rocky Mountains. Taking in the splendor and majesty of God's creation was as natural as breathing. I was always looking heavenward. It didn't matter if I was walking outdoors, driving the car, or enjoying the indoors, I was looking for those mountains in reverence, worship, and awe of God's creation. That's where I truly learned how to worship. Ever since my personal mountain splendor experience, I've been on a quest to learn all I can by reading, studying, and asking God to show me how to authentically worship Him.

For too long, worship has been misunderstood. Worship should never be limited to the music we sing or hear in a church service. Worship is bowing down with our entire lives before the God of the Bible, the God of creation. The leper fell on his face in worship to God (Luke 5:12). The women at the empty tomb, when she they saw Jesus, bowed and held his feet in worship (Matthew 28:9).

Oh, how I wish I could hold his feet. But I can bow down, in my living room, kitchen, and in the middle of His creation. I find joy just as great when I'm worshiping prostrate before Him and He whispers His love to me. *"How great is the love the Father has lavished on us, that we should be called the children of God"* (1 John 3:1). As much as I love to sing, when I am in deep worship, I can't sing, I can't speak, I can only whisper and tell God how much I love Him.

A.W. Tozer wrote, "Worship is an everlasting preoccupation with God." That will be our great joy and role in heaven, worshiping Jesus. Right now, here on earth, is our rehearsal. What are rehearsals for? To get it right. Tozer had it right. That's my heart's cry to be preoccupied with God in worship. I want to hear Him when He whispers to my heart and when He does, I whisper back to Him.

I think worship is in my DNA. I think about it all the time. More importantly, I want the people around me to share the same wonder of God in their everyday lives. Is it time to be quiet, on your knees or flat on your face before God? Are you ready to be so in awe of Him alone, that you can't audibly speak, just whisper? It is a great quiet place to be. Let's join the leper down on our faces before the King of kings, and the women who clasped the feet of the resurrected Savior for the very first time. Then whisper a word . . . a single word or short prayer.

May my meditation be pleasing to Him,
as I rejoice in the Lord."
Psalm 104:33-34

Donna Fagerstrom, author and speaker, has served in the local church, seminary leadership, and discipleship ministries. Every Mourning (2018) has circulated over 38,000 copies in both English and Spanish. Her most recent book, Lifted (2020 release) is for those who struggle with life issues. Being a wife, Mama and "Nonna" is her great joy.

A Christmas Lesson

Tonia Gütting

Yes, my husband asked me, and yes, I agreed. It seemed like an okay idea back in the fall. But now the realization of not one Christmas tradition being upheld while on the road sent me into all stages of grieving. Bless the U.S. Army's little heart, we had a winter move. Then to top it off, we were to perform for a friend's wedding the day after Christmas. That held the promise of some snow in Pennsylvania's hills instead of the Sandhills of Fort Bragg, North Carolina. But, we couldn't get home. Nor could we get a home at our new duty station, so why not? Seize the day! Except, not Christmas Day.

As usual, I hadn't thought this through particularly well. My husband realized we needed the car space, so gifts were opened a couple nights before in a small, moldy military lodging room that smelled of dog. After the excitement, the kids mournfully packed the gifts back up for storage until we returned. No decorations. My man could only take so much Christmas music in the car. We arrived in the dark to a little town of Pennsylvania—not Bethlehem—to find a Super 8 with a window facing a tired gas station. Only a skiff of snow covered the accumulation of the fall's soot. I can't remember if everyone else was crabby, but I know I was. This was not how Christmas Eve was supposed to be.

Christmas Eve, in my world, was supposed to be the most holy night of the year. You are supposed to go joyfully but reverently to a church service and light candles and sing. Then you go to your home, eat soup and cookies, and sit around the fire with hot chocolate. The excitement is supposed to build till you can't stand it and you lie in bed awake half the night.

Yet, on this eve my man herded us back into the car and onto the highway to a rocking diner/bar—it's very neon sign an obnoxious beacon into the grey night. It was loud and busy. The young waitresses draped their arms over the old men's shoulders, laughing loudly at their old jokes. The men cheerfully handed out large-bill tips in return.

I perfected my scowl through the burgers and shakes, but no one seemed to notice I'd become the Grinch in the corner. I refused to acknowledge the community in this truck-stop Christmas Eve "church."

By Christmas morning, it became apparent I should have been more grateful for the now-closed diner. We trudged across the parking lot to the gas station for breakfast and lunch. Let's see, hot dog or microwaved burrito?

As the day wore on, our friends realized we were already in town. They hadn't expected us, weren't planning on us. They explained that they were staying with her sister, but she was fine with it, so would we come to dinner? No really, they always have room for extra guests. Truly, they'd love to have us.

So, we herded back into the car and drove through the dark streets with its dark windows and closed doors. Eventually we found the open door at the top of the hill at a three-story Victorian with its light spilling out through the windows.

Of course, there were swags and lights and a perfect tree. The kids took off with new friends and into rooms full of toys. The fire warmed what had been cold for days. The other guests were a mix of several facets of our host's lives— the old widower who was their neighbor before moving to the nursing home, friends from church, one of their employees.

As we sat down at the old oak table, the gift further unwrapped itself. We found our hosts were owners of the local bakery—chefs who loved food, who had planned and practiced and perfected for this performance. Courses paraded out from the antique behemoth stove. The meal took hours and proved so much more than it was *supposed* to be.

You can draw several morals from the story—that Christmas isn't about my golden traditions, that I need to be flexible, that I should trust God when He puts me someplace, that I shouldn't let a move happen until after December 25. But don't miss the most obvious one: that a selfish, undeserving, crabby stranger with nothing to give is invited to the extravagant, opulent, overflowing table. From the shepherds at the manger to the thief dying beside Him on the cross, this is what Jesus did His whole life. He invited the unlovable to the feast.

He continues to give the invitation.

His grace still overwhelms.

Tonia Gütting is a freelance writer, a church planter with her now-retired U.S. Army Chaplain husband, mom to three young adults, and St. Francis to two dogs and a salty cat. She loves all things outdoors where God reveals His beautiful, powerful, intricate, complex, glorious self. She blogs about these things and more at: https://sabbatics.wordpress.com.

Mashed Potatoes Are Good and So Is God

Cynthia B. Holloway

One particular Thanksgiving Day was unlike any other I had ever experienced, and it had everything to do with mashed potatoes. I love mashed potatoes, but my father-in-law loved them even more. Imagine my disappointment when I found out that the restaurant I had reserved for Thanksgiving dinner this particular year would not be serving mashed potatoes on their elaborate buffet. When I made the reservations, I jokingly asked if I could (BYOP) bring my own potatoes. Afterwards, the more I thought about it, I said, "Why not?" I got excited just thinking about surprising my father-in-law with a bowl of spuds after he had filled his plate with all the traditional Thanksgiving foods. We were a small group of four this year. My mother-in-law was opposed to going to a resort restaurant for Thanksgiving, but for some reason she relented and agreed.

It had become a tradition over the years on both sides of my family that I mash the potatoes, and to this day I am unsure why. This Thanksgiving I was excited to mash the spuds, but I had no idea it would turn out to be a true God moment. Through the restaurant I trotted with my hot spuds in tow and my family none the wiser of the secret surprise I held in my large purse.

Sure enough, as my father-in-law made his way around the wonderful array of food, he filled his plate, sat down and said, "Well, there is everything here but the dumplings and mashed potatoes."

I happily said, "Well, I don't have dumplings, but I have mashed potatoes," and with excitement I produced the spuds. The look of surprise on everyone's faces was worth the embarrassment of sneaking the potatoes in. As we enjoyed our meal, our waitress approached our table and was perplexed to see our plates arrayed with a scoop of white creamy potatoes. I shared about sneaking the potatoes in, and she thought it was pretty funny and also commented how many other people in the large dining room were wishing for potatoes; no one could explain why there were no mashed potatoes on the buffet. We had a good laugh and continued our meal.

As we enjoyed our dessert, the hostess approached our table and wanted our opinion regarding our dining experience. My father-in-law proceeded to tell her how wonderful everything was, now that he had had his potatoes. We told her our story, and she proceeded to say that the question of the day had been, "Where are the mashed potatoes?"

The hostess also mentioned that one family was particularly upset. I immediately asked her to point the family out to me. Without hesitating, I lifted the bowl of potatoes from my purse and made my way to the middle of the dining room where they were seated. I jokingly said, "I hear you would pay a high price for some mashed potatoes." As they looked at me completely speechless, I began to get a little embarrassed that I had interrupted their meal. The gentlemen and his wife just stared at one another and finally after much coaxing on my part, I convinced them that I really did want to share my potatoes with them.

The man asked me, "Where did you come from?" I replied, "From across the room, I'm having dinner with some of my family." "How come you have a bowl of mashed potatoes?" he asked. I explained that when I called ahead to make a reservation I asked about the menu and learned there would be no mashed potatoes. I wanted to surprise my family because mashed potatoes were a favorite of ours. The wife listened quietly and never said a word except a quiet, "Thank you" when she scooped the potatoes onto her plate. I wished them a Happy Thanksgiving and made my way back to my seat. I felt good about sharing my spuds but felt something seemed a bit uneasy with the family.

After my family and I finished our coffee, the lady who had hesitated at taking my potatoes began to make her way to our table. She approached me, looked me in the eye, and said, "You were so generous to share with us, I now feel compelled to share with you." She was shaking and noticeably upset. In her hand she held a photograph.

She began by saying that the picture was of her son. In May of this year, he had taken his own life on the eve of his eighteenth birthday. She went on to say that Thanksgiving had been his favorite holiday, and that last year before his death they had entertained a very large crowd of family and friends. This was their first Thanksgiving without him. They could not bear the thought of being home for the holiday, so they had packed up for the weekend and were staying at the resort to have Thanksgiving dinner alone with their younger son.

The lady went on to say how terribly disappointed she and her family were to go through the Thanksgiving buffet and find that there were no mashed potatoes. For you see, mashed potatoes had been their son's favorite all-time, anytime food. Her son's love for mashed potatoes was even talked about during his eulogy. They were not even sure they could make it through their meal, that was how upset they were to learn that there were no mashed potatoes. Her last words to her family before leaving their New Jersey home was that they would eat plenty of mashed potatoes on Thanksgiving Day and think of their son. The family was shocked I had approached them bearing mashed potatoes.

After she shared her story, there were lots of tears. Her husband joined us, and we were all in awe of what had transpired over the last few minutes. Finally, I said, "You know this was not about our family having mashed potatoes for Thanksgiving, but it is about God's personal message to you." I told them I believed God wanted to give them hope and encouragement during their grief, and that I truly believed God wanted to assure them that their beloved son was in His presence and doing just fine. It was affirmation for them as well, as they tearfully received God's message.

It is pretty amazing when you think about it. Our family dining out on Thanksgiving was certainly not the norm. For me to inquire about the menu ahead of time and make the potatoes was also unusual. To have an employee who was not even our waitress tell us about a family who was particularly upset and to choose the one family out of 150 other guests to share with were all acts of Divine Intervention.

As I have shared my story of faith with you, I hope it has caused you to reflect on your own life where you could see God's grace at work in your life. Do not be too quick to count things that happen as just a coincidence. God doesn't work like that, but he does work through willing hearts and obedient servants. Learn to listen to that still small voice deep inside, you know, the voice that gets you excited about something; that is God's way of speaking.

As believers, God has given us the gift of the Holy Spirit. The Holy Spirit prompts us to do those things that bring Honor to God. The mashed potato sharing was not about *me*, but it was about God, who loved this grieving family enough that He wanted to encourage them, and He did it through a bowl of mashed potatoes. We serve a *big* God . . . and He works in powerful and awesome ways.

I'll never look at a scoop of potatoes without being reminded of God's unpredictable and sometimes humorous ways. For the grieving family, the encounter got them through Thanksgiving, and they have referred to that day as their "miracle day."

Just a few weeks before Thanksgiving, I had been praying about something personal in my life and asking that God would use me to make a difference. God showed me that He can use me wherever I am. All it takes is a willing heart. For you see, I was serving up mashed potatoes, and God was dishing out blessings. Mashed potatoes are good, and so is God!

Cynthia Holloway has a passion for helping women grow in their faith. She is the founder of a ministry group which hosts six events a year, and she leads Bible studies, counsels' others, and is writing a devotional book. Cynthia is married and resides in Maryland with her husband and an adorable cocker spaniel.

Thus Far

Sandy MacMillan

Then Samuel took a stone and set it up between Mizpah and Shen. He named it Ebenezer saying, "Thus far the Lord has helped us."

1 Samuel 7:12

I was on the phone with my counselor—yet again—detailing the most recent circumstances that had my family in crisis mode. Over the past several years, more than a few challenges had threatened my family's security, health, or finances, if not all three. I felt guilty about the number of times I called my counselor after hours so she could talk me through "what if" scenarios and remind me that, whatever happened, God would be with us.

It was truly hard to see God's presence in the midst of these struggles. I had prayed for years about the challenges at their center. I had fasted. I had claimed promises from Scripture. And I had prayer walked around the significant people and places in our lives. Yet, it seemed like instead of getting better, things were worse. The miracle I believed God for seemed far away and less possible than ever.

Yet this time, as I spoke with my counselor and thought about how many times we'd been through similar phone calls, something new occurred to me. I realized that, while our family had faced more than our share of challenges in recent years, the fact that we were bracing for a new crisis meant that we had made it through the previous ones. We had survived the storm thus far.

Thus far. These two words hung in the air as I remembered how the prophet Samuel set up a memorial, calling it Ebenezer, or Stone of Help, and declaring, "Thus far the Lord has helped us."

Samuel set up his memorial after God granted the Israelites a decisive victory over the Philistines, their longtime territorial rivals. The Israelites had faced their own crisis when, as they gathered for a prayer meeting, they discovered that the Philistines were gathering for war. Samuel prayed on the Israelites' behalf, and God intervened, throwing the Philistines into a panic that sent them running.

The Israelites' success, as decisive as it was, was just one battle in their ongoing conflict with the Philistines. There would be more crises for the Israelites, just as there had been multiple crises for my family. Samuel knew this victory wasn't the end of their struggles, but he also knew that celebrations should not wait for final victories. He knew a key truth I had missed, the need to celebrate what God has done "thus far." Samuel knew, if the Israelites would celebrate the ways God had helped them along the journey, they would grow in faith and learn to trust God for the individual successes that lead to final victory.

When we are faced by a crisis, it's easy to fall into one of two traps. The first is to get lost in the weeds of worry. We get so anxious about the terrible things that *could* happen, that we don't appreciate the good things that *do* happen. Our worries blind us to the ways that God provides for us, guides us, and keeps us safe one day at a time.

The second trap is the tendency to look only for big once-and-done miracles. We hope and pray for God to miraculously calm the storm, heal the relationship, or multiply the loaves and fishes. We long for God's abundant grace to sweep through our lives and heal our hurts all at once.

But most of the time, God's grace comes in whispers, gently guiding us through the storm rather than calming it.

Most of the time, God's grace grants us one small victory at a time, as it teaches us to rely on God's sufficiency each day. If we only look for the big miracles, we miss the miracle that God has helped us through, thus far.

When we take time to look for the ways God has been with us *thus far*, when we listen to the whispers of his sufficient grace, everything changes. We begin to recognize that the God who has been with us in the past continues to be with us in the present. We notice the ways God helps us day by day. And we grow in confidence that tomorrow, and the day after that, we'll again be able to say, "Thus far the Lord has helped us!"

Oh God, you who are our Ebenezer, we thank you that thus far you have helped us. Enable us, we pray, to see the ways you give us victory each day, to lean into your sufficient grace, and to hear its ongoing whisper, "Thus far!" Amen.

Sandy MacMillan is a women's ministry leader who helps people find encouragement in God's Word and works to connect hurting people with sources of help and hope. She is pursuing a doctorate in pastoral counseling and loves family time with husband, Jim, their two grown sons, and her two daughters-in-love.

Love Saturated Bonuses

Crystal McFadden

Do you hear it? Better yet, do you feel it? There is an ever-so-slight, still, small voice that will lovingly interrupt the very direction of your day. Do not miss it! In less than a micro-second, this interruption of knowledge is drowned out by the noise of this world without a trace, so much so that we immediately begin questioning if there was really an interruption in the first place. The impact is there and gone so quickly that, if left unnoticed or ignored, seamlessly slips through the creases of this broken world without a trace. Odd.

Why so dangerous? Why would something so subtle and barely noticed be forced out of our sight so quickly? Why the need to quench our attentiveness toward God's whispers of wisdom and love? Why would such a message, a prompt, a guidance so subtle, be worth the effort of removing all traces as suddenly as it arrived?

The magic of this moment comes from the Maker Himself. This undeserving, yet freely extended conversation is a gift for those who trust and believe in Jesus. In the Old Testament, the Holy Spirit would come upon humans like that in Isaiah 59:21, but in the New Testament, the Holy Spirit guides those who love, live for, and put their trust in Jesus (see Matt 10:19-20, Mark 13:11, Romans 8:26-27, 1 Cor 2:13, 12:7-11, Gal 5:25, and more). God's adoration and attentiveness toward us can leave us enamored. Knowing Him leaves us only one desire — to seek after Him, cultivate a deeper reverence for Him, obey His direction excitedly, praise Him, and live for Him while we await His return. Do you notice a trend?

The attention on God and the exchange of love and light, truth and action with God, crushes all aspects of darkness and depravity regarding our separation from God. Darkness is powerless against God's victory and will do anything to remove signs of His love in order to grapple for moments of attention and our focus. Darkness knows that if our attention is on the things of this world, we will naturally veer from the goodness and promises of God. The enemy knows that those who are not for God, are against Him (Matthew 12:30, Luke 11:23). Unfortunately, those who are not holding tightly onto the truth and redemptive blood of our Savior can feel bombarded and helpless as they are consumed with insecurity, instability, and confusion set up by the distractions of this world. The battle leaves us feeling overwhelmed, isolated and inwardly focused rather than the truths that God is with us and has already won over sin and death.

When believers realize we have the freedom to cultivate a watchful eye, anticipatory ear, humble heart, and a posture of obedience to our Lord, evil itself shudders at the thought (Matt 7). Believers must pay attention to these whispers to navigate the noise of this world. What if we all intentionally sought out His truths to guide us? Wow. Look out world!

By God's grace, because of Jesus' death and resurrection–we have been gifted an opportunity for adoption and oneness with our Lord for eternity. Intimacy is desired from the depths and beginning of our existence. All creation groans for His return, but our yearning does not create an automatic intimacy (see Romans 8: 15, 19-23). Intimacy is developed when we begin a lifestyle of proclaiming, *Yes God! I am here, send me!* This is similar to Samuel's response in 1 Samuel 3:10, "Speak, for your servant is listening." Intimacy comes with commitment from our eyes, ears, heart, mind, and body (see Matt 22:37, Luke

10:27). Obedience breeds opportunity. It is in our obedience that seemingly ordinary days begin to exhibit the extraordinary moves of love from our intentional and creative Maker.

His calls and our obedience form a life posture pleasing to Him. Those whispers of grace birth the divine intimacy between the Holy Spirit and the visible lives of believers. Even Jesus expresses that it is for our good that He had to leave because we would receive our helper, a gift from Him, that He would always be with those who believe (see John 16). Jesus' love and obedience to the Father was a model for us. The gift of the Spirit is a victorious force, unmatched by anything or anyone in all of creation. God is on the move and has invited, allowed, and encouraged His beloved to be a part of this story for His glory (see 1 Cor 10:31).

Applying His Truth and adhering to these whispers of grace can change the dynamics of our hearts, our homes, and even our nation. It creates a response unlike those of this world. It proves the dichotomy between our Holy God and our sin nature. The world will still be broken, we are all still sinners in need of a Savior, but the lens in which we take in our data has been exchanged. The way in which our God sees us has been replaced. In Christ we are a new creation (2 Cor 5:17), adopted into His family (Eph 1:5, 2:19), co-heirs with Christ (Rom 8:17), and now set forth on mission to love God and love others until we return home (Matt 22: 37-40, Mark 12:30-31).

Receiving whispers of His grace, His mercy, His love and His truth affirms in our hearts that His presence remains. He is with us (Joshua 1:9, Is 41:10, Matt 28:20). He has created us to live on mission during our time here on Earth (Matt 28: 19-20). These opportunities to hear and to follow are the gifts allowing our steps to form us more into His likeness.

I will never forget the evening my husband and I were addressing a very sensitive and life changing topic. I remember having been an emotional wreck for days, fasting and praying, crying and wailing, when no one but God was there to see my emotions "work the crazy" out. The topic had me in a tailspin. The anxiety was more than I could bare. The night came where we had a window of opportunity to chat, and I obeyed God's call to take it. With calm, soft, direct, Biblical and assertive posture I began to speak. I paused often to breathe and stayed relentlessly prayerful in my heart as words somehow arrived coherent out of my mouth.

I'll never forget the words I heard, "Wow. You did that well. I was hoping you'd make it easy for me, and I could just get up and have the excuse to walk away. Yet, by saying all that in the way you did, I'm here. I'm listening. I'm not going anywhere." This event was guided by repeated whispers of grace by the Holy Spirit. God showed off as he began a path that formed both unity and respect, laughter and a deeper love for one another, while receiving all the credit for anything good blooming in our home and family. Neither of us *deserves* to have a partner who chooses to love and work, learn and grow together. We are all broken humans and will choose ourselves if left to our own will. We simply have been given the opportunity to know the God whom we serve in deeper ways, in order to love those He entrusted us to love and grow with. Good seasons are not necessarily for us, but to point and show off His glory. God's grace saturated the conversation that evening and many conversations moving forward. It was by adherence to His Truth and the attentiveness to His still, small voice that we continue growing closer as one. We communicate better than ever before and choose to give love rather than expect it. By God's lead, we continue to learn.

Please do not mistake my message, God's whispers are not magical dust that make things easier, simpler, or even "right." They simply equip us with His Truth to guide our choices. His whispers are gifts on top of the salvation He's already given that which we cannot earn for ourselves. The payment of our sins which has already been done, that we do not deserve. These whispers will always align with what Scripture teaches, the character of God shown to us in the Bible, and the resources He has made available for the journey. He does not promise to shelter us from pain or tears, death or trial, He simply identifies the path to become reconciled with Him for all of eternity and the grace to be forgiven and choose Him over and over again.

He is enough. His whispers of grace are simply love saturated bonuses.

Crystal McFadden, LPC, is a speaker and writer. She is owner of Crystal Cnvrstns, LLC ("Conversations"), wife, mom, military veteran and military spouse. Crystal is on mission to serve others and glorify God by blending her expertise in the fields of resiliency, professional poise, mental health, and Biblically based living as they relate to God's design of our body, brain, and heart.

Jesus and the Amygdala

Marmi B. Molloy

Unusual title, I know. Jesus and Mary Amygdala? Jesus and the merry amygdala?

Actually, I am talking about part of the brain's limbic system, the amygdala. It is located in the feeling-part of the brain. Along with other functions, the amygdala detects threat and is key in our response to fear—Freeze, fight, or flight. The amygdala can work in sync with our relationship with Jesus to help us react in healthy ways when we are triggered by fear.

The last assignment for a six-week outpatient mental health program I attended the summer of 2017 was to write a letter to yourself. Mine started, "This five-year mental health journey started with Jesus telling you, "Don't be afraid; just believe." You are a wounded, scarred warrior. He (God) designed you to be on the front lines, but not to fight every battle. Choose your battles wisely. Most battles are fought on your knees, not with your aggressive mouth…" I then listed things I feared, the worst of which was my children not coming out of the shadow of death alive.

In the midst of my struggle, God used the story of another fearful parent whose twelve-year-old daughter walked in the shadow of death.

The gospel of Mark, chapter 5, tells us a crowd has gathered around Jesus on the shore. Jairus, a leader of the synagogue, is there. He falls at Jesus' feet, begging Him to come to his home where his twelve-year-old daughter lies dying. Jesus departs with Jairus. The crowd follows, too.

A woman in the crowd interrupts them along the way. She had been suffering from bleeding for as long as Jairus' daughter had been alive. She spent all her money on doctors who only made things worse. She heard about Jesus and thought to herself, "If I can just touch his clothes, I will be healed." She touches. Jesus whispers a miracle. Her bleeding immediately stops. She falls to her knees in front of Jesus. Jesus calls her "daughter" and says, "your faith has healed you. Go in peace and be freed from your suffering."

At the same time Jesus was speaking to the woman, messengers arrived and told Jairus not to bother Jesus anymore because his daughter had died. But Jesus heard what the messengers said. He ignores them and speaks directly to Jairus, "Don't be afraid; just believe." Jesus does not let the crowd follow except for Peter, James and John. At the house, there is another crowd of loud mourners gathered. Jesus again makes them leave. Jesus took those three disciples along with Jairus and his wife into the room the little girl was lying in. And then, another whispered miracle. Jesus holds her hand and says, "Talitha, koum" (which means "Little girl, I say to, get up!"). Immediately, life returns to the twelve-year-old girl. She stood up and walked around!

Could these quiet miracles break the grip fear had on me? How do I cultivate the faith of the bleeding woman? How does one not be afraid and just believe?

DO NOT BE AFRAID

Philippians 4:6 is the classic verse for anxiety. It directs us to not be anxious, to pray, and to receive the peace of God that will guard our hearts and minds. This magnificent prescriptive verse is preceded by an essential truth. The phrase right before, "do not be anxious" says, "I am near (*eggus* in the original language)" (Philippians 4:5b). The

Greek adverb *eggus* means near in place and/or time.* It is the presence of Jesus that empowers us to live out the following exhortations to be mature, righteous believers by not living in anxiety. I think knowing *Jesus is near* is the key to not being afraid.

I picture the no-longer-hemorrhaging woman approaching Jesus in fear when asked to reveal herself as the toucher-of-the-cloak. I see Jesus embracing this "unclean" woman, publicly declaring her to be His daughter, obliterating her isolation and fear. Jesus ends her suffering and sends her off in peace.

I picture Jesus putting Jairus' face between His hands, His eyes seeing deep into Jairus' trauma-triggered brain (amygdala) saying, "Ignore them, I've got you. I'm right here with you. I didn't forget about your daughter while I was ministering to another. Don't be afraid. Believe ME. Trust ME. Have faith in just ME."

JUST

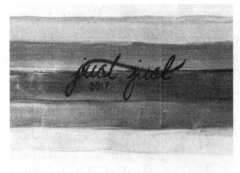

Why did he add "just?" He could have said, "Don't be afraid, believe."

Knowing Mark 5:36 was a significant verse I clung to for my mental health, my daughter created this profoundly simple painting. She affirmed my need to "just, just." When the fears attack, I *just* be still and know He is God. I don't fear, I *only* believe.

Like Jairus, we must ignore what others say and *just* listen to Jesus. Like the woman, we need to ignore the crowd and seek Jesus.

BELIEVE

I remember the visceral pain I felt when my children were in the shadow of death. Groaning in the spirit with Gethsemane-take-this-cup-from-me type prayers. Don't be afraid; just believe. Believe what?

In her book *Letting Go of Worry, God's Plan for Finding Peace and Contentment*, **Dr. Linda Mintle writes, "trust is an act of faith — it is believing God when the evidence does not support His goodness. Faith says He is good no matter what we see in the moment."

Dr. Linda Mintle also talks about training our brains and the role of the amygdala. She has enormously helpful "worry-free exercises" at the end of each chapter for the body, soul and spirit. She states, "If we trust Him, are obedient to His words, and ask for wisdom, worry has to leave."

My oldest son created my favorite piece of art to date. He titled it "Two Perspectives of the Devil." The girl is his sister. Jesus has taken her hand. "Little girl, get up!"

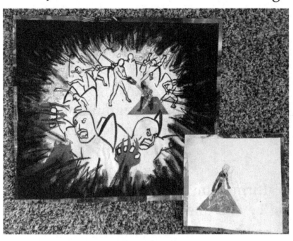

When I first saw it, I thought the tiny black dot in the bottom right of the smaller image was a smudge. He explained that the spiritual warfare battle depicted in the larger portion is actually happening in the little dot. Perspective. Truth is his sister is firmly standing upon her rock and when compared to Jesus being near, the enemy is just a small, conquered speck.

So, what about Mary Amygdala . . . I mean Mary Magdalene? She was one of the women most devoted to Jesus. Jesus had miraculously healed her and "clothed her in her right mind." She (and the "other" Mary) were the first at the empty tomb. The two women were "afraid yet filled with joy" as they followed the angel's instructions to tell the others He was risen. Along the way, they see their beloved, resurrected Jesus. He tells them not to be afraid; go and tell.

Likewise, we are frightened but also filled with great joy. We limp...walk...run...We go and make disciples of all the nations, assured He is always with us, to the very end of the age.

Scripture taken from the HOLY BIBLE, NEW INTERNATIONAL VERSION Copyright 1973,1978,1984 International Bible Society. Used by permission of Zondervan Bible Publishers.

* Bible Hub *"Near" in place or time "eggus"*

**Dr. Linda Mintle http://drlindamintle.com/books/

Mintle,Linda, *Letting Go of Worry*, p.75, Harvest House Publishers, Eugene, Oregon 2011

Mintle,Linda, *Letting Go of Worry*, p.212, Harvest House Publishers, Eugene, Oregon 2011

Two Perspectives of the Devil, by Ryan Brown, rgbrowndesign@gmail.com

Marmi B. Molloy is the pen name for Margaret. Marmi is her Indonesian name. She lived and labored there for eleven years. B is for Brown, her last name during her twenty-seven-year marriage. Molloy is her maiden name. She has three amazing adult children.

Becoming a First Fruits Woman

Danielle Porter

Honor the LORD with your wealth and with the first fruits of all your produce; then your barns will be filled with plenty, and your vats will be bursting with wine.
Proverbs 3:9-10

I became obsessed with the concept of "first fruits" in 2017 when I was sitting in my Bible study leader's house. I was sharing how I had been challenged in my health coaching business to begin waking up early and devote time to a "morning process." One of the women in our group asked, "Where is God in all of that process?" It began as a simple question, but led me to understand there should be more to my morning process than mere routine.

In an agriculture-based culture like that of the Old Testament, first fruits meant something quite different than it means today. During harvest time, it's time to reap what you sowed. You gave your first fruits to the priest (Leviticus 23:10) as a sign of faith; a sign that you trusted that God would provide, not only economically but also for you and your family's daily sustenance. Moses first brings up the idea of first fruits in Exodus, and then the Bible goes on to mention it twelve more times. So, it's obviously something God wants us to take note of. Just like when you repeat yourself over and over to your children, you want them to take notice. God is that way too.

The concept of first fruits is so easy to dismiss as an "Old Testament colloquialism" that doesn't apply to 21st century people like you and me. I mean, it's a safe bet that you don't harvest crops from your backyard from which you sacrifice the first fruits from. However, we do have something precious to offer. It's something everyone, from your kids to your spouse to the random strangers on the Internet, are clamoring for—your time and attention.

While we might not have grain or wine, oil or honey, in our back yard to sacrifice, we do have something incredibly precious, our time and attention. From the moment our eyes flicker open, our time and attention are in demand. It goes from our alarm clock, to—let's be honest—our phone that's already muddied up by those little red notification buttons. They demand we click and see what happened while we were sleeping. "You have 18 unread emails and 4 direct messages waiting to be seen!" they scream. On top of that, if we're in a life space where we're constantly awakened by a baby or toddler, it's obvious where those screaming demands are coming from. Our time is so often not our own, unless we make a conscious intentional effort to set aside that time as a sacrificial offering to God.

Personal development gurus will tell you that the first hour of your day is the most important. They say "successful" people don't give other people the first hour of their day. Successful people use that time to pour into themselves so they can show up as the best version of themselves. They do this so they can sell the most real estate or face cream or even simply become the most patient Mother. And I totally agree, we need to fill our own cup first. Yet, what if instead of pouring into ourselves from a cup that will always run dry (the world's cup), we have the choice to pour into ourselves from God's cup? The cup that never runs dry.

Sacrificing our time and attention, before it is sullied by the demands of others, gives God first dibs on us. And doesn't He deserve that? After sacrificing His son as first fruit (1 Corinthians 15:20), doesn't He deserve the first fruit of our day?

Danielle Porter is a woman, mother, Christian, sinner, friend, and a health coach. Struggling with her weight and self worth most of her life, she entered the health and wellness field. She has found that physical health and your walk with Christ are intertwined and seek to expose their interdependency.

Strong Winds

Lisa Rose

Sometimes it seems that the chaos that is life turns us in an endless circle. The wind intensifies, and it is all we can do to stay standing. We wonder, how did I end up here? What happened that put me into this whirlwind of stress and worry and uncertainty? Did I miss the turn off? Was I blazing through my life so unaware that I completely missed the neon sign blaring:

WARNING, STRONG WINDS AHEAD - TURN HERE

Surely there must have been one, there must have been a detour somewhere. Because surely this was not God's plan for my life. We don't like to imagine that this difficult section of the road was, in fact, exactly where God intended our life to be. Here in the storm, in the midst of uncertainty, we learn trust. We learn that there is only one who can really guide our path.

Trust His heart for you!
Trust His Love for you!
Trust His plan for you!
He will not fail to pull you through the storm!

Lisa Rose lives with a heart to encourage others. As a Christian who loves hugs, lavender roses, and her sweet rescue dog, Pepper. Lisa enjoys writing about the love of her Heavenly Father. She shares her journey of her over one-hundred-pounds of weight loss and encouraging words at www.arosehug.com.

The Power of Sabbath: Whispers of Grace in a Time of Rest

Debbie Culver Sanders

For me, listening to the sweet whispers of God is about learning that His loving arms offer us rest. One of the biggest steps of my faith journey is in my trust that God desires for me to rest in Him alone and, from this deep trust I am called to enjoy the day of rest known as the Sabbath. Hearing this gracious whisper of rest and Sabbath hinges on our faith in God, the Father, Son, and Holy Spirit. We do nothing to deserve it or earn it. This is God's whisper of grace given to all of us to enjoy and to embrace. Resting in the arms of our gracious God is about our trusting Him and enjoying His offer to rest.

For some Christ followers, the practice of Sabbath may stir feelings of concern and apprehension. The very use of the word of Sabbath is unfamiliar to many of us. Possibly, we may have questions flooding our heads and hearts like, "What exactly does it mean to practice Sabbath?" "What day is the Sabbath?" "Does the practice of Sabbath rest take us back to living under the law of the Old Testament?" "How do we practice Sabbath rest?" "Is this a burden too heavy for us and discouraged by the Bible's words of grace?" "Will I stop listening to the whispers of grace with this practice?"

While working through my graduate degree at Judson University in ministry leadership, I was invited to consider the Sabbath along with other concepts of rest like retreats and sabbaticals. Knee-deep in enjoyable research, I was struck by the beauty and the gift that followers of Jesus have been given in enjoying a day of rest called Sabbath. The research helped me to recognize that this offer of rest is not, in fact, about burdening ourselves with rabbinical rules or laws about how many steps one could take in a day, thus constituting burdensome labor. In addition, it does not involve finger pointing of judgment on those that did not practice rest the way I understood the scriptures to communicate. Instead, I came to understand that this is about trust and freedom. I was wrapped in the arms of our loving God with encouragement to trust and to enjoy the grace He is offering me with the biblical practice of Sabbath. The rules are not the issue. Grace is what I was encouraged to embrace and to savor. I am continually learning to hear God's whispers of grace to me as I consider Sabbath rest.

The Dance of Grace

It seems to me the more Christians get to know the love of the Trinity, the more we realize we have been offered an invitation to a 'dance of grace.' In this dance, I am held in the arms of the all-powerful Creator and I experience the permission to accept I have limits while also being His beloved child. My imagination places me on the ballroom floor of a tale like Beauty and the Beast. With no effort, I am guided across the surface by the gentle embrace of the Lover of my soul. I can hear the gentle whispers of His love and delight for me. I am not required to clean myself up or get my act together. I merely trust that I am His beloved. His grace and His mercy cover me like a beautiful ball gown spun by the Savior's great sacrifice and perfect love of me.

While intensely personal, I am also aware there are many others on the dance floor being led by the same Gracious Lover, and it is marvelous. The music of this dance of rest and grace flows to each of us every day. Furthermore, with gentleness and kindness, the music of Sabbath rest summons my acceptance by this Grace Whisperer, the King of kings,. He knows who I am. He made me with limits and desires. He delights in giving me boundaries because I'm created to need rest and times for reflection and renewal. This King knows I have many weaknesses and needs, so He leads me beside still waters (Psalm 23). There is nothing hidden from Him. He knows me completely (Psalm 139:13-17).

Rest for Our Soul

I have a feline friend named Cleo (short for Cleopatra). She is the queen of the house, or so she thinks. She naps whenever she wants and wherever she thinks it is comfortable. She prefers to prowl around the house at night searching for mice and other distractions. When morning comes, she informs me of her hunting success and tells me it is time to feed her. And next? She curls up somewhere and takes a nap. She has limits. She does not need to work all day and then collapse. She eats, drinks, hunts, and naps. She is my cat, and I am her human. I know this because, while she takes her evening nap, she lays on the back of the sofa and puts her paw on my shoulder. She lets me know she is there, and I am hers, and she is mine. She is content and at peace with her life. There is no other place she would rather be in her world. I ask myself—Do I purr with great satisfaction about my life? I want to purr like Cleo. I want to place my hand on God as I rest, knowing that I am his human and He is my Father (Isaiah 43:1). God's whispers of grace proclaim to me that I am His child, He knows me, and He knows what I need.

Perhaps this is the human challenge—knowing our limits. Do we know what we need and what our purpose is? Do I understand this about myself? I now know a little better that I am called to love the Lord and to enjoy Him forever; that I am the beloved of the King of kings. I show my enjoyment of God in many ways, but particularly in showing my enjoyment demonstrated in my trusting Him more and more. My life is learning to listen to His whispers of grace that invite me to consider what He is offering me. I am learning to hear His words of love and hope despite the hardships of life and shifting seasons.

Practicing Sabbath rest is our way of knowing who we are and whose we are. In the very beginning, the Creator showed us the beauty and gift of Sabbath rest. In Genesis, we read about God making all of creation, including human beings on day six. Then before we humans did a day of work, God proclaimed the seventh day our day of rest. Think about that. We had not done any work or proved our worth in any way, but God said, "Let's begin with rest; simply being together." Sabbath is not something we earn after six days of work. Sabbath is an invitation to embrace the limits and enjoy the Creator and His creation. From the beginning, Sabbath has been a grace whispered.

Practicing Sabbath takes awareness. The intentional times of practicing Sabbath rest help us to adjust our hearing for His music of grace, for the whispers of grace. The daily pauses point us to His beautiful will that our life is not about earning His grace. His whispers invite us to listen generously — to cease striving and to be still. "Cease striving and know that I am God; I will be exalted among the nations; I will be exalted in the earth. The Lord of hosts is with us; the God of Jacob is our stronghold. *Selah*" (Psalm 46: 10-11, NASB). Did you know that Selah means "pause?"

Sabbath is a song that encourages our efforts away from trying to get attention and to win approval through our own effort. It is about knowing that each day has enough worries of its own, while the whispers of grace from God are calling us to enjoy the rest, to embrace the limits and to listen to the whispers of His grace.

Do you hear the call from our Creator to rest? Can you actually hear His whispers of grace? Will you hear the music playing an invitation for you to be open to dance with the

Lover of your soul, the Grace Whisperer? Why not try embracing the power of Sabbath rest with me and many others? There's infinite room on the dance floor.

After many years of pitching her tent in foreign lands, Debbie Sanders now resides in rural Virginia at The Shepherd's Tavern. She is a spiritual director, enjoys slow dancing with husband, Dave, and is the mother of adult daughters who are helping her learn to play and dance with her grandchildren.

Living Parables of Central Florida, Inc., of which EABooks Publishing is a division, supports Christian charities providing for the needs of their communities and are encouraged to join hands and hearts with like-minded charities to better meet unmet needs in their communities. Annually the Board of Directors chooses the recipients of seed money to facilitate the beginning stages of these charitable activities.

Mission Statement

To empower start up, nonprofit organizations financially, spiritually, and with sound business knowledge to participate successfully as a responsible 501(c)3 organization that contributes to the Kingdom work of God.

GPS Grant Program

GPS–Godly Positioning System—helps charities and non-profits position themselves, through our business coaching and the supply of grant funding, so they can succeed long-term in fulfilling their callings to minister to the unmet needs in their communities.

Made in the USA
Middletown, DE
25 November 2020